Soul of a Diamond

Heart-Centered Women Sharing Stories of Resilience and Joy

Sanet Van Breda

Diamond Beauties Forever

NATALIE MCQUEEN • GIOVANNA TARTARONE • CINDY EDINGTON
JENNIFER ROGERS • ANJANA LALA • JULIE DIAZ • CHRISTA ROSE
ROBYN EYRE-LONG • SUZI DENT • DONNA SPARACO MEADOR
DAR GEIGER • SONÉ SWANEPOEL • VAL BURGESS • LS KIRKPATRICK
ANGEL MARIE MONACHELLI • DR. ALEXANDRA MCDERMOTT
CHRISTINE J WILLIAMSON • MARIE BAILEY • MARY J ROBINSON

Soul of a Diamond: Heart-Centered Women Sharing Stories of Resilience and Joy
Published and distributed in Scottsdale, Arizona, Gifts of Legacy LLC

Print Paperback – ISBN: 979-8-9898500-8-2
Print eBook – ISBN: B0D6D7WNZP

If you would like to do any of the above, please seek permission by contacting Gifts of Legacy via email to GiftsOfLegacy@gmail.com
Publisher: Gifts of Legacy LLC
Language: English
Editor – Buddy Thornton
Marketing Team – Perfect Publishing
Copyright 2024, Sanet Van Breda. All rights reserved.

PerfectPublishing.com

Acknowledgements

I extend my deepest gratitude to all those who have contributed to the realization of this project. First and foremost, I am immensely thankful for the divine presence that guided me through moments of uncertainty and bestowed upon me the vision for the 'Soul of a Diamond.'

To my family and friends, your unwavering support and encouragement have been my rock throughout this journey. Your belief in me has fueled my determination to turn dreams into reality.

A heartfelt thank you to the incredible women whose stories grace the pages of this book. Your courage, resilience, and vulnerability have illuminated the path for others to find hope and inspiration.

Thank you to my beautiful Aaron Heimes, the President of E360tv, for loving my vision and granting the Soul of a Diamond TV Show. Special appreciation goes to the incredibly talented Mujahid Nisar for his exceptional artwork and banners for the shows.

I am immensely grateful to my Editor-in-Chief, Soné Swanepoel, for her invaluable contributions to the artwork in our beautiful Diamond Moments Magazine.

Heartfelt thanks to Natalie McQueen from Gift of Legacy for sponsoring the shows and for collaborative editing efforts alongside Buddy Thornton on all the chapters in the book.

A sincere acknowledgment to Perfect Publisher's Dr. Ken "Smiley" Rochon, Ed Colwell, and Al Granger for making this outstanding God-Given Project a reality.

To the readers who embark on this journey with us, thank you for allowing these stories to touch your hearts and minds. May they inspire you to embrace your own journey of resilience and empowerment.

Last but not least, to the electric eel that appeared as a symbol of divine intervention, thank you for sparking the flame of creativity and guiding me towards the path of transformation.

With deepest appreciation,

Sanet Van Breda

Table of Contents

Sanet Van Breda – Kaleidoscope of Dreams.................. 1

Natalie McQueen – Put Your Super Cape on With
   Me & Let's Create Legacy................................... 15

Giovanna Tartarone – Rainbow Promise:
   A Journey of Soul Awakening During Adversity........... 27

Cindy Edington – The Long Road to Discovering "Me"...... 39

Jennifer Rogers – Rise of a Phoenix......................... 51

Anjana Lala – From People-Pleaser to Self-Love:
   Anjana's Journey of Unbecoming.......................... 63

Julie A. Diaz – Rock your Health Journey!.................. 75

Christa Rose – Live The Life You Love 87

Robyn Eyre-Long – A New Perspective..................... 99

Suzi Dent – Age-Defying Confidence:
   The Power of Self-Belief at Any Stage 111

Donna Sparaco Meador – How to MasterDate™ -
   Thriving After Loss or Divorce 123

Dar Geiger – Being God's Joyologist...................... 135

Soné Swanepoel – Voiceless No More..................... 143

Val Burgess – From Captivity to Compassion:
   Lessons from Leonard Robinson 155

LS Kirkpatrick – My Four Super Powers 163

Angel Marie Monachelli – Ignite Your Ultimate Energy,
Joy, and Abundance 175

Dr. Alexandra McDermott and Jae Wilcox –
How a Mother and Daughter Combine to Create
the S.O.U.L. of a Diamond 185

Christine Jaya Williamson – The Secret Scared
Garden Space 193

Marie Bailey – From Sorrow to Sunshine................... 201

Mary J Robinson – The Heart of a Woman 213

About the Author 225

Radiant Heart

Poem by Sanet Van Breda

Moments of moving from there to here
Between the star and the moon's soft glare
Capture a glimpse of light so rare
Radiant and shining, our hearts declare
For the world to see, in love's grand affair
Moments of our lives that are filled
With laughter keep us going, hearts thrilled
Capture the essence of who we are
In the spirit of a child, like a shooting star
Moments to share our true stories, so bright
Not only for the world to heal, take flight
But to remind us how amazing we are
Forever moving forward, a radiant star
To create magic, near and far
In the radiance of each heart's sweet glow
We find the strength to carry on and grow
Shining bright, our love does show
In every moment, from dusk to dawn's soft flow
Radiant hearts, we shine so bright
In the diamond moments of love and light
Together we rise, our spirits take flight
In the beauty of each day and every night

Foreword

My dream of becoming an author has been my driving force for the past two years. While I had collaborated on a few books, the idea of penning my own work was deeply ingrained in my aspirations. However, when my initial experience didn't unfold as I had envisioned, I found myself grappling with disappointment. I vividly recall one of my lowest moments, sitting beside a serene river in South Africa, tears streaming down my face as I questioned why things hadn't gone according to plan.

It was June 25, 2023, a day when my heart felt heavy with discontent. Amidst my emotional turmoil, a miraculous sight unfolded before me: an electric eel emerged from the water, its sleek form shimmering in the sunlight. At first, I questioned whether my tears were playing tricks on my eyes, but as I watched the eel gracefully navigate the currents, I felt a profound sense of clarity wash over me.

At that moment, it was as if the universe was speaking directly to me, offering a vision of hope and possibility. From the depths of my despair emerged the inspiration for 'Soul of a Diamond'—a vision encompassing a television show, a magazine, and a compilation book. The electric eel, with its enigmatic presence and electrifying energy, became a symbol of resilience and transformation, igniting a spark within me to embark on this incredible journey of creativity and empowerment."

As I pen these words, reflecting on the journey that brought us here, I am filled with gratitude. Gratitude for the miracles that punctuate our existence, for the moments of despair that lead to divine inspiration, and for the opportunity to share this journey with you, dear reader.

May the pages that follow serve as a beacon of hope, a testament to the resilience of the human spirit, and a reminder that even in our darkest moments, miracles await, ready to illuminate our path forward.

With love and boundless gratitude,

Sanet Van Breda

Chapter 1

Sanet Van Breda

Kaleidoscope of Dreams

As I stand here, enveloped in the quiet embrace of my surround-
ings, I sense something stirring within me. At first, it's just a subtle
whisper, a gentle nudge from the universe. But then, an electrifying sensation courses through me, setting my hair on end and
sending shivers down my spine. With eyes closed, I surrender to
this newfound energy pulsating both around me and within me.

In an instant, it happens. A kaleidoscope of vibrant colors bursts forth, casting a radiant glow that dances across my skin. I feel its warmth on my face, its gentle caress on my throat, and its comforting embrace around my heart. It's an undeniable sensation, one that fills me with awe and leaves me longing for more. At this moment, I am bathed in the light of possibility, my spirit alight with the promise of dreams yet to unfold.

Unbreakable, Unbelievable, Unstoppable; Wow, what do these words have in common? Me!

At the end of each day, I ask myself, "Sanet, did you leave your sparkle in someone's heart and memory today?" And with my whole heart, I believe that I do. I really do. It's funny; I feel a surge of love every time I repeat those words, reminiscent of the two "I do's" I uttered—once when I got married 34 years ago and again atop the Empire State Building when I received a call to action from God. I fervently prayed for the opportunity to pick up my grandsons from school every day and to be the kind of grandmother who dances, plays, and nurtures their imaginations for as long as possible. This desire, deeply rooted in my heart, was now being answered by a journey I had been on with God for the past few years. I was ready and open to whatever He had in store for me.

While I stood in line to enter the Empire State Building, the atmosphere was filled with cheerfulness and happiness. Despite it being six days into 2022, people were still wearing their masks with a sense of joy. I eagerly awaited our turn to go inside; it had been a lifelong dream of mine ever since I watched "An Affair to Remember" with Cary Grant and Deborah Kerr. Back in 1976,

South Africa had just begun its television journey, and I can still remember our first set—a simple black-and-white model. In the early '90s, one of my favorite movies, "Sleepless in Seattle," featured an unforgettable romantic scene atop the Empire State Building. As I stood in line, I couldn't help but wonder: would the view be as breathtaking as it was in the movies? And perhaps, just maybe, would I encounter my favorite movie moment come to life?

The history and interconnectedness of the Empire State Building's journey to the top was truly inspiring. Even the elevator operator wished me a wonderful experience as we ascended. As I reached the summit, the scene before me took my breath away, and I could feel my core temperature drop by 10 degrees. Feeling frozen, I leaned against the wall and looked upward, wondering where the warmth emanated from. Suddenly, beams of redness enveloped me as if they were saying, "Lady from South Africa, you are really not dressed for New York's January weather. Let us warm you a bit." Grateful for the unexpected warmth, I hesitated to wear my husband's thick archery jacket, which proudly displayed "South Africa Archery" on the back. After all, South Africa had recently been removed from the red list, having been labeled as the originating country for the Omicron virus back in November 2021.

Standing underneath the beaming sunlight, I offer gratitude to my beautiful God for the love and grace He bestowed upon me on the 6th of April 2019. That day, I marked a pivotal moment—a point of no return—when I decided to embrace life rather than succumb to its weight. It was a profound shift, igniting a commitment to move more than I consumed. Dancing on my Forever

Song *Walking On Sunshine* by Katrina and the Waves every day, and on some days, five to eight times. What followed were months and years of the most tumultuous roller coaster ride of my life. I clung to God's promise that He would support me while I, in turn, vowed to do whatever it took to shed the weight of an entire person. Some days were easier than others; some were impossibly heavy, requiring me to navigate through each minute, each moment, with relentless determination.

The battles waging within my mind seemed endless, echoing doubts of whether this struggle would ever cease. Yet, despite the relentless onslaught of doubt and the mind games I endured, I pressed on. I persevered, steadfastly following my Oumie and Zander Plan (Oumie being "granny" in my home language, *Afrikaans*, and Zander being my grandson). Two and a half years later, I emerged victorious—I had shed the weight of an entire person. But it wasn't just pounds I lost; I gained so much more: strength, resilience, and a profound sense of pride in myself and my ability to take action, speak out, and bravely face challenges. Self-respect, self-love, self-discipline, and self-belief—all the "self" elements—became integral parts of my life story and my mission to share with the world. I learned that by infusing yourself with self-love and mindfulness every day, you can accomplish anything and conquer everything. My incredible journey and transformation are detailed in my book, "Flight of the Monarch: The Hero Inside Me.

Standing in the warmth of the beaming heaters, I gazed down at the buildings and the tranquil Hudson River, enveloped in the symphony of laughter echoing from those who were also experiencing this breathtaking panorama. With my heart overflowing with longing, I closed my eyes and offered a prayer to God, praying to Him for a miracle to fulfill my deepest wish—to be reunited with my beloved grandsons. My soul yearned to live each day with purpose, to serve others in every way possible. Over the past five years, I have found my voice and embraced my worth, experiencing a profound transformation that has altered the course of my life forever. My greatest desire is for others to encounter this miraculous journey of self-discovery and empowerment that I have been blessed with. I am driven by a passion to showcase the inherent value of every individual, to assure them that their stories are significant and worthy of celebration.

God answered, "Open your eyes; you will inspire so many people around the world." As I opened my eyes, my heart nearly stopped at the sight before me. It wasn't the buildings or the Hudson River; it was millions of people looking at me. Overwhelmed, I forgot to breathe, tears streaming down my face. "Yes, my beautiful Lord, I am ready to fulfill Your God-given plan," I whispered. "Thank you for trusting me. I do, and I will take action every day."

With blurry focus, a gentleman approached, asking if I was okay. Nodding, I wiped my tears and snot with the underside of my blouse. As I looked into his eyes, he reassured me, "Everything is going to be okay." In Afrikaans, he added, "Alles wat jy daar sien gaan waar word!" Shocked, I realized his words affirmed my vision. Tears flowed again, for the second time in three years, as God silently promised my dreams of becoming a hands-on granny and living in my purpose, Serving with Love, would come true. With this incredible miracle unfolding before me, I am compelled to step up and transform my vision into reality, making my dream of creating my vision "To be earth's most heart-centered brand and to provide experiences that fill the world with love, joy, and happiness!".

In the first sentences, I have used three words, and the first two words show you what happened and why I wanted to become UNSTOPPABLE.

With my newfound truth and understanding, I've come to realize that every encounter with another person holds profound meaning. It's an opportunity for me to leave a glimmer of my sparkle and to experience the unique brilliance of others—their wisdom, dreams, and individuality—each day. Embracing authenticity and staying true to myself, I continued on my God's Quest, on a journey filled with gratitude during my six-month stay in America. I'm deeply grateful to my sister and brother-in-law for graciously hosting me during my travels, allowing me the space to connect with others and explore new horizons.

In this spirit of connection and empowerment, I took the first step towards manifesting my vision by transforming my beloved Diamond Beauties Forever ladies' group. What began as a WhatsApp group of 79 women evolved into a private Facebook community—a sacred space where ladies come together to inspire and uplift one another through life's highs and lows. It's a testament to the power of sisterhood and the resilience of the human spirit, where women from all walks of life can find solace, support, and strength in each other's presence.

As I witness the bonds of sisterhood deepen and the flames of inspiration ignite within our group, I am reminded of the profound impact that one small step can have. By listening to the whispers of my heart and acting, I've created a ripple effect of love and empowerment that extends far beyond my wildest dreams. It's a beautiful reminder that when we align with our true selves and trust in the guidance of a higher power, miracles unfold, and our vision becomes reality.

What steps could you take when you want to become Unstoppable? I have a Miracle five-step plan that I would love to share.

5Steps2beUnstoppable

Step 1 – Clarify Your Why:

Your why is the driving force behind your actions, the fuel that propels you forward even when faced with challenges. Take a moment to deeply reflect on what truly motivates you, what ignites your passion, and what you're willing to do anything and everything for. In both of my transformative plans—Oumie and Zander Plan (Lifestyle Change) and now in my SLIM Plan—I have anchored myself in my why. I've defined my goals and aspirations, painting a vivid picture of the results I strive to achieve.

As you set your sights on your journey, consider your principles and values. They serve as your guiding compass, keeping you aligned with your true path. Imagine your journey as a bridge spanning from where you currently stand to where you aspire to be. Envision the Golden Gate Bridge in San Francisco stretching out before you—a magnificent testament to possibility and adventure. Though the path ahead may seem daunting from your vantage point, trust that once you cross the bridge, you'll behold a breathtaking vista that awaits you on the other side.

Step 2 – Dream in 3D:

One of my favorite steps on the journey to becoming unstoppable is to dream in 3D. This transformative practice costs nothing and yet yields priceless rewards. Over the past three years, I've discovered the power of dreaming with all my senses, bringing my visions to life in vivid detail. Picture yourself in a grand movie theater, the screen illuminated before you. You're not just a passive observer; you're the leading actress, experiencing every emotion, sensation, and moment within the film.

As the story unfolds, you feel the rush of excitement, the warmth of love, and the thrill of adventure coursing through your veins. Then, with a shift in perspective, you step outside the confines of the screen, immersing yourself in the world you've created. It's akin to stepping into a painting and exploring its depths from every angle. (One movie that depicted this immersive experience was "Inception," where characters entered dream worlds within dream worlds, blurring the lines between reality and imagination.)

Step 3 – Designing your Blueprint:

To design your blueprint for success, it's essential to set SMART goals. Break down your vision into specific, measurable, achievable, relevant, and time-bound objectives. By doing so, you provide clarity and direction to your journey, enabling you to focus your efforts and track your progress effectively. For example, suppose your ultimate goal is to start your own business. In that case, your SMART goals might include tasks such as completing a business plan within three months, securing funding within six months, and launching your product or service within a year. Each goal is clearly defined, with measurable milestones that guide you toward your overarching vision.

Another crucial element of designing your blueprint is cultivating a growth mindset. Embrace challenges as opportunities for growth rather than setbacks. Adopt a mindset that views failure as a stepping stone to success and believes in your ability to learn and improve. This shift in perspective empowers you to overcome obstacles with resilience and perseverance. Instead of being discouraged by setbacks, you see them as valuable learning experiences that propel you forward. With a growth mindset, you approach each challenge with optimism and determination, confident in your ability to adapt and thrive in any situation.

Continuously seeking knowledge and developing new skills is a cornerstone of designing your blueprint for success. Invest in personal and professional development opportunities that are relevant to your goals. Whether it's taking courses, attending workshops, or seeking mentorship, prioritize learning and growth as integral components of your journey. For instance, if your goal is to advance in your career, you might pursue certifications or training programs that enhance your skills and expertise in your field. By expanding your knowledge base and honing your abilities, you position yourself for success and open doors to new opportunities.

Step 4 – It's All in the Action:
In the pursuit of your goals, taking consistent action is paramount. Break your goals down into smaller, manageable tasks and commit to acting towards them every day. While progress may seem slow at times, each step forward brings you closer to your vision. By consistently showing up and putting in the work, you build momentum and make steady progress towards your

desired outcome. Whether it's dedicating a set amount of time each day to work on your goals or completing specific tasks, consistency is crucial for achieving success.

As you navigate across your Golden Gate Bridge towards becoming unstoppable, it's essential to embrace resilience. Setbacks and obstacles are inevitable along the way, but it's how you respond to them that matters most. Cultivate resilience by bouncing back from setbacks, learning from failures, and adapting to change. Instead of allowing challenges to derail you, view them as opportunities for growth and learning. Embracing resilience enables you to persevere in the face of adversity, ultimately strengthening your resolve and fortifying your commitment to your goals.

Surrounding yourself with positive, supportive individuals is essential for staying motivated and inspired on your journey. Seek out mentors, coaches, and peers who believe in your potential and encourage your growth. Surrounding yourself with a supportive network provides you with valuable guidance, encouragement, and accountability. Whether it's seeking advice, sharing successes and challenges, or simply receiving words of encouragement, having a supportive community by your side can make all the difference in staying focused and motivated toward achieving your goals.

Step 5 – Celebrate Small and Big Achievements
Celebrating all achievements, regardless of their magnitude, is a crucial step in the journey towards becoming unstoppable. With each milestone reached, I weave celebrations into my goal-planning process. Whether it's something as simple

as treating myself to an ice cream cone or as grand as splurg-
ing on a new dress, I ensure that I acknowledge and honor my
progress and accomplishments. It's not just about celebrating
the end goal but also embracing the journey itself—the trials,
triumphs, and everything in between.

As I pursue my goals with unwavering determination, I recognize
the importance of prioritizing self-care. Taking care of my physical, mental, and emotional well-being is essential for sustaining
momentum and resilience on my journey. I make it a priority to
engage in self-care activities that recharge and rejuvenate me,
enabling me to show up as my best self each day. Whether it's
spending time in my hydroponics garden or simply taking a few
moments to meditate, practicing self-care allows me to nurture
myself and maintain balance amidst life's demands.

In the ever-changing landscape of life, remaining flexible and
adaptive are essential skills for navigating challenges and seiz-
ing new opportunities. I embrace an open-minded approach,
willing to adjust my plans and strategies as needed to overcome obstacles and pursue my goals. By staying flexible and
adaptive, I empower myself to respond effectively to change
and uncertainty, ensuring that I can adapt to whatever comes
my way with resilience and grace.

Finally, it's essential to acknowledge and celebrate your wins,
no matter how small. Each achievement, no matter how seemingly insignificant, is a testament to your progress and dedication. By recognizing and celebrating your successes, you
reinforce positive habits and bolster your confidence, fueling
your momentum on the unstoppable journey ahead. Whether

it's sharing your achievements with loved ones, treating yourself to a special reward, or simply taking a moment to reflect and express gratitude, celebrating your wins is a powerful way to honor your journey and inspire continued growth and success.

The greatest lesson I've learned on my journey to becoming unstoppable is this. When I wholeheartedly commit myself to a cause empowered by unwavering determination rooted in my "why," I am unstoppable. Through consistency, perseverance, and an unshakeable belief in myself, I've come to realize that the realm of possibilities knows no bounds. As I continue to embrace each challenge as an opportunity for growth, celebrate both small victories and significant milestones, and nurture my mind, body, and spirit with self-care, I stand emboldened and validated by the profound truth that anything I set my mind to is within my reach.

Your power and wisdom are always within you; you need to delve into the depths of your heart and soul. Begin with your purpose and your why, and dare to dream big, bold dreams. Then, take decisive action to become the person you aspire to be. For me, this journey of becoming means embodying the voice of millions, creating space and platforms for extraordinary souls to illuminate our world with their brilliance, wisdom, and transformative stories. Through my Your Voice TV Network, Diamond Moments Magazine, and summits, I strive to empower individuals to share their voices and shine brightly, making a meaningful impact on the lives of others. Join me in embracing your inner power, unleashing your potential, and making your dreams a reality. Together, let us inspire, uplift, and create positive change in the world.

Golden Nugget

> "If your WHY is big enough you will
> do anything you will do everything!"

About Author:

Name – Sanet Van Breda

Contact – https://www.selflove4me.com

President of Your Voice TV Network / Producer / Publisher / Author / Speaker / Mentor.

The voice of millions, providing space and stages for extraordinary souls to illuminate our world with their brilliance, wisdom, and transformative stories across all my platforms, TV shows, Diamond Moments Magazine, Soul Diamond Publishers and MWAH Production. My mission is dedicated to empowering communities, particularly Diamond Beauties Forever and Tanzanite Heroes.

Chapter 2

Natalie McQueen

Put Your Super Cape on With Me & Let's Create Legacy

Your life can change in a minute. No, in a second. I experienced a terrifying event that changed the trajectory of my life forever—a near-death experience where I saw my entire life flash before my eyes. I was beyond grateful that I survived this event, and the experience became the source of my biggest blessing in disguise. Surviving influenced me to rethink my life's mission and purpose.

Seven years ago, my wake-up call experience changed my life. After all, I was staring death in the face. My mind flashed through visions of my husband, children, parents, and my brother, plus all the special moments I might miss out on. My motherly wisdom would never be shared with my daughters for their good or bad days or during their important future events.

A few weeks after being rescued, I began to envision other mothers and their legacy. What about the mom who received a diagnosis of cancer and had six months to live? How could these women, or any parent who wanted to create a legacy of memories for their children, be served? This gave me a crystal-clear vision of the inspirational message that I wanted to create to inspire others on their path of leaving a legacy through living the life they were meant to live.

My name is Natalie McQueen, Founder of Gifts of Legacy and My Talking Journal, a 10-time International Bestselling Author, Legacy Speaker, book publishing and marketing expert, and a Certified Coach in Mindset Mastery. I was born and raised in Northern Ontario, Canada, where I met my husband, who became my childhood sweetheart in the summer after eighth grade. Through 33 years of love and marriage and raising two beautiful daughters, we have experienced many memorable moments. My daughter Taylor is 27 years old, and Kayla is 25 years old.

We always created many family traditions as a group. Whether it was the special-shaped birthday pancakes made for them or the frenzy of decorating the Christmas village, the girls always knew their mom was there for them, and there wasn't anything I wouldn't do for them. We were kind of a crazy family that loved adventure and had many fantastic times together.

My motto is always, "Try your best to live life to the fullest." My family always joked that I could make friends at the grocery store check-out or in line at Disney Land. By the time we were at the front of the line, I was inviting them to visit us.

My company, Gifts of Legacy, was born out of this. Through this soul-felt transformational experience, I created a treasure trove of opportunities for mothers to share their traditions, dreams, wisdom, and voice with their children, grandchildren, and great-grandchildren. I started creating products and systems that guided families to leave video messages, pictures, memories, and traditions in either a book, workbook, or journal format to be uncovered by future generations.

At this point, I was scanning the marketplace to see what other products existed out there that were like mine or like all the ideas I still had in my head. I found very few products, and when I found one, I would see all the things they forgot to account for.

I felt a slight stir in my stomach, and I wondered why there weren't products like this. I could not be the first person to think about this. Then the fear rushed in that maybe I should stay in my lane of publishing and forget about creating these other unique products. At that point, I stopped and reminded myself that I was given a second chance in life for some reason.

Maybe my mission in life is to make it easier for people to document their journey of life so that it can be shared and safe for generations. So, from then on, when I got that scared feeling of doing something out of my comfort zone, I imagined that I had a Super Cape with Bling Sparkling Letters on it that said, "Super Legacy Creator." And when I had that cape on, I was protected and could feel powerful and listen to my instincts, knowing it was going to be fantastic. I would be the Superhero to help others Create, Live, and Preserve their Legacy.

I have partnered with a company that has helped people store documents for over 100 years. This allows someone who wants to leave all their family photos organized in sharable folders to do so. They require a beneficiary to preserve the legacy and ensure access to the account. To facilitate this, I help families organize their storage system.

I serve mothers who could leave a voice recording for their children for many birthdays and other occasions. I love helping the mom who may only have six months to live. She could still have an impact after she is gone by reminding them of her proud feelings and love. The vision is to create timelessness so those in the present can project into the future and be entirely present for loved ones with all a mother's unique love brings to the table.

My passion is to reach the everyday person who has all their photographs piled up in boxes and empower them to become intentional about creating their legacy and avoid losing all those endearing memories in a fire or flood. They can incorporate all kinds of memories, such as love letters, keepsakes, family recipe books, legacy messages, and more.

Here are some of the questions I ask those who are beginning their legacy journey:

- Do you wish there was a step-by-step blueprint on how to leave an impactful legacy for your family?
- Are you worried that if something happened to you right now, your essential documents and final legacy wishes would not be created, updated, and protected adequately?
- While taking your last breath in this world, would you like to feel you have lived each moment to the fullest, following your desires, dreams, and passions, and have no regrets?

Sometimes, a single moment can change your whole life. Yes, that's what happened to me. One incident gave me a whole new mindset, which shifted my life's purpose. Let's pivot and consider this perspective.

We all have a purpose in this world. We can develop by learning, experiencing, teaching, and introspection. As we do this, we can share our wisdom and knowledge to help develop others. If your purpose is to be a stay-at-home mom, then be the most "bad-ass" stay-at-home mom you can be! If you choose to be a janitor, then be the most reliable, friendly, life-loving janitor you can be! There is no judgment or shame for what you choose if it feels fulfilling to you.

We are not all meant to be brain surgeons. We each contribute with our God-given gifts and each action we take! However, like in the movie Groundhog Day, we can feel like we're on the hamster wheel of life. We continue the same routine, day after day, unaware that we can create a new reality.

When I started to look at my life, I realized I was the 'Yes' gal and wanted to help everyone. Even when it took up time, I could have been doing things that I was much more passionate about. I was using my precious time doing things for others while they were out living their passions.

I also knew I was avoiding putting myself out there because of fear of failure and possible judgment. I knew I had to tell my story to help others from ever feeling as unprepared as I had after my near-death experience. We accept whatever happens, and that doesn't feel genuine to me.

I am now living my passion by encouraging others to live out loud, intentionally, and freely, fulfill their Legacy List, and create the life they love most. I have a Facebook group called **Creating Your Legacy Life,** where I share tips on Creating, Living, and Leaving your Legacy.

What I love the most is interviewing people from all over the world, finding out how they are living their best lives, and helping to make the world a better place. I love learning from others and getting to understand their unique family traditions and wisdom.

When we can learn about others' differences, we can celebrate with them instead of being afraid of them. I genuinely believe the world's people have so much more in common as far as wanting to achieve their passions and being loved by their families.

I created a Legacy List workshop to assist people who were looking for answers. I created separate sections to dream in and assess how satisfied they are with different areas of their lives.

I've divided those sections into:

- Accomplishments & Attributes
- Relationships & Environment
- Career & Mission
- Travel & Experiences
- Time & Money
- Physical & Mental Body
- Lifestyle & Giving Back

I found many benefits to creating my Legacy List and wanted to share this with others. It helps them to focus on what they truly desire in life, analyze where they are now, and where they want to be. Your Legacy list contains everything from the steps toward goals, a potential list of desired achievements, activities, and experiences, to trips they'd like to take.

When we look at the legacy list items we want to achieve, it can look scary if we don't know how to complete those tasks or don't have the money to go where we want to go. This is where thinking of putting on that Super Cape comes in very handy. The Super Cape symbolizes heroism, virtue, and courage. Whenever we think about mythical heroes, we imagine them wearing capes as they swoop in to save the day or stop whatever is in the way of achieving the superhero's goal.

When paired together, the Super Cape evokes power and strength, making the superhero feel unstoppable. This is what we need to do in our lives.

I call my Bucket List my 'Legacy List' because it encourages me to think, plan, and implement steps to bring my goals to fruition. When I first made my Legacy List, I wrote down everything I could think of in each category. I used my computer to research travel ideas. I believe we don't let ourselves dream big enough. Don't hold yourself back.

One of my favorite quotes is by Les Brown: "The graveyard is the richest place on earth because it is here that you will find all the hopes and dreams that were never fulfilled, the books that were never written, the songs that were never sung, the inventions that were never shared, the cures that were never discovered, all because someone was too afraid to take that first step, keep with the problem, or determined to carry out their dream."

Another comes from Eric Micha'el Leventhal: "The closer you come to knowing that you alone create the world of your experience, the more vital it becomes for you to discover just who is doing the creating." Eric's quote hinges on the experience. Experience is not what happens "to" you; it is what you learn from the events. You alone decide what is worth learning. I am so passionate about empowering others to create their legacy now and not put off what can't wait.

Life is so short, and we may never have the opportunities of the present again. Deciding on your legacy starts today with the gift of the present. So, when it comes to legacy, here's a quote to live by: "Never regret a day in your life: good days give happiness, bad days give experience, worst days give lessons, and best days give memories." Unknown Author

Focus on feeling gratitude for everything as often as possible. I look for gratitude in my day because it keeps me grounded in the present. I pray for you to embrace the same. Enjoy the present and invite in a feeling of inner peace. It's okay to take a deep breath. Go ahead. Soak in that good feeling. Allow yourself a pause time. Doesn't that feel good?

Recognize the role you play in your life. When you can step up and take full responsibility for what is going on, it can be life-changing! When life doesn't work out as planned, it is easier to blame other people and circumstances. However, when you take responsibility for guiding your path and for where that path takes you, then you set yourself up for success instead of failure and disappointment.

"It is only when you take responsibility for your life that you discover how powerful you truly are." Allanah Hunt

What I've learned is that everything I have done up until this point in time has placed me precisely in my present situation, whether good or bad. I found my power when I chose not to spend two minutes making excuses or dwelling on the past! Doing that will only make you feel like a failure or guilty that you've made bad choices in your past. Let go of blame. Stop it!

Susan V. Bosak uses an analogy for leaving a legacy like tree roots. She talks about where to find the best place to plant a young tree. Is it in a clearing, within an old forest surrounded by other trees, or in an open field?

According to ecologists, a young tree grows better when it's planted in an area with older trees. As Bosak says, "The roots of the young tree can follow the pathways created by former trees and implant themselves more deeply. Over time, the roots of many trees may graft themselves to one another, creating an intricate, interdependent foundation hidden under the ground. In this way, more robust trees share resources with weaker ones so that the whole forest becomes healthier.

That's legacy: an interconnection across time, with a need for those who have come before us and a responsibility to those who come after us." I realized that my story is Important! It will guide others to a pathway to create strong roots interwoven in their own families. Ultimately, we should strive to be like trees, creating strong vines and roots for our future, intertwined with our past generations.

So, stop procrastinating and jump into the life you were made to live. Pull out your Super Cape with me, and you, too, will be unstoppable at creating your best legacy.

Golden Nugget

"Don't leave a mess, Leave a Legacy!"

About Author:

Name – Natalie McQueen

Contact – https://giftsoflegacy.us

Natalie McQueen, Founder of Gifts of Legacy & My Talking Journal, has brought over 1400 authors to #1 International Bestseller status, including a series endorsed by Mark Victor Hansen. A 10-time Bestselling Author, Natalie wrote *Gifts Of Legacy: The Ultimate Blueprint for Generations to Enjoy*. As a Legacy Designer, she helps people share their life stories in Legacy books, business books, anthologies, and memoirs. Natalie created My Talking Journal, featuring 3-minute recorded inspirational messages from entrepreneurs and small business-es, to inspire daily writing. The journal includes 90 other messag-es, encouraging people to write and share their legacies.

Chapter 3

Giovanna Tartarone

Rainbow Promise: A Journey of Soul Awakening During Adversity

In Genesis 9:13-16, God makes a covenant with Noah after the flood, promising never again to destroy all life on Earth with a flood. The sign of this covenant is the rainbow: "I have set my rainbow in the clouds, and it will be the sign of the covenant between me and the earth" (Genesis 9:13, NIV). It serves as a reminder of God's faithfulness and his promise to be with us, even during difficulties and storms. This passage illustrates the enduring love and grace of God towards humanity.

My story surpassed the boundaries of my personal journey; it evolved into a beacon of inspiration and optimism for countless souls confronting their own adversity. It serves as a testament to the unwavering human spirit to overcome, transform, and inspire.

My journey had its origins in my early years as an Italian-born immigrant who settled in the United States during my childhood. My parents had dreams of creating a better life for their family, and I wholeheartedly embraced the opportunities that my new home offered.

As I grew, so did my ambitions. I pursued a career in finance, eventually working with prestigious Fortune 100 companies. On the surface, my life appeared successful, but beneath the facade of achievements, I felt a profound sense of unfulfillment.

The turning point arrived when personal hardships struck my life. My son faced health challenges that tested my faith and resilience. The devastating loss of my mother to cancer deepened my understanding of the fragility of life. These heart-wrenching experiences had a profound impact on me, igniting a realization within me that change was necessary. My path to becoming a symbol of strength was not without its trials and tribulations.

Determined to make a difference, I shifted gears and pursued a career in education. I earned a second master's degree in special education and became a dedicated teacher for children with autism.

But life had more challenges in store for me. In 2015, I faced the heartbreaking loss of my father, followed by a devastating diagnosis of breast cancer in 2017.

It all began with a life-altering phone call—one that nobody ever hopes to receive. It was the moment when I was diagnosed with breast cancer, I will never forget the day I received that cancer diagnosis on April 14th, 2017. I felt like I was handed a death sentence.

I remember going into the closet, closing the light, and asking God, "Why me?" and "What have I done to deserve this?" All I heard was, why? Now, I look back, and I know deep inside why I got cancer. I smoked to release the stress of my daily obligations. I had poor eating habits because I was always on the run and deprived myself of sleep. I had to study for school and take care of my family. I really did not treat my mind, body, and spirit well.

Cancer: A diagnosis that would forever reshape the course of my life. In the wake of this news, I found myself engulfed in a whirlwind of negative thoughts and paralyzing fear. Throughout my cancer journey, my mental state held a tight grip on my life, consumed by the relentless fear of dying.

Every doctor's appointment and every test I underwent filled me with dread, anticipating more bad news with each visit. I vividly recall the day I visited a renowned hospital to consult a top doctor for a lymph node biopsy. The anxiety and stress were so overwhelming that I always cried on the way there. Days later, I received a call informing me that they had missed the lymph node and needed to repeat the test. I was trapped in a dark and terrifying mental space.

The thought of leaving my children without parents, given my mother's passing at the age of 30 and my dad's passing at age 45, filled my heart with an unending pain that I could never bear. I didn't want my kids to experience the same anguish. The only thing I knew at this point was to turn inward and for God to lead the way as I promised: I would change my life if he would grant me a second chance.

My faith in God was strong; I chose to believe and act as if my second chance was granted. I was grateful for all the simple things in life. I began to google how to be positive with a cancer diagnosis, which led me to embark on a journey of self-discovery and transformation.

As an educator, I delved into the study of the mind, seeking to apply the knowledge I had gained. I conducted extensive research and read "The Biology of Belief," which inspired me to make a profound decision: Changing my beliefs about cancer would be my driving force for surviving cancer.

It was the one aspect of my life over which I could exercise absolute control. Through rigorous research and the application of mindset principles, I began to reshape my thinking about my health. The most significant lesson I learned from this process was that our thoughts, which stem from our beliefs, profoundly influence the experiences we encounter. Even amid the darkest moments of my journey, I embrace my newfound glimmer of hope and an unwavering determination not to let cancer define me or dictate my future.

I understood that the battle I faced was not solely physical but deeply intertwined with my thoughts and beliefs. At this point, my faith was stronger than my fear. This realization marked the inception of my transformation.

My background in mindset work, acquired through my previous work, became a cornerstone of my healing journey. It was a journey that I embarked upon with an open heart, inspired by my son's health challenges and my deep empathy for students with autism. I believed that shifting beliefs was the key to empowerment and positive change.

Driven by this belief, I delved into the works of renowned thought leaders like molecular biologist Dr. Bruce Lipton and Dr. Joe Dispenza. Their teachings illuminated the intricate connection between our thoughts, beliefs, and our physical well-being. I realized that by reshaping my beliefs, I could not only transform my reality but also inspire others to do the same.

I remember watching this video in which Dr. Dispenza stated that if our mind can make us sick, then is it possible it can make us well? This question opened my mind to the possibility of finding out the answer to my mind's capabilities.

My transformational journey began with immersing myself in studying how to take control of the mind with the teachings of many spiritual leaders. These experiences compelled me to delve into personal growth with my late mentor Bob Proctor and Napoleon Hill's work, leading to discovering the remarkable capacity for resilience, inner strength, and overcoming limitations within the human spirit. Inspired by my deep belief in the spirit-mind-body-spirit connection, I further explored the realm of energy medicine.

The path to transformation was not without its challenges. I viewed my cancer diagnosis as a wake-up call—an opportunity to rediscover my true purpose in life. With unwavering determination, I embarked on a mission to rewrite the narrative within my mind, recognizing that this inner transformation was the key to my survival.

Seven years later, I stand proudly as a cancer survivor. My passion for serving others burned brighter than ever. I had unlocked the profound wisdom of the spirit-mind-body connection, and I was determined to share this precious knowledge with the world and help others who are touched by a cancer diagnosis.

Drawing from my love for rainbows, which symbolize hope, healing, and transformation, I crafted the RAINBOW framework—a self-empowering wellness journey.

Let's break down each step of your R.A.I.N.B.O.W framework:

1. **Reconnect with self:** This step involves reconnecting with one's true self, perhaps through introspection, meditation, or self-reflection. It's about understanding who you are at your core and what truly matters to you.

2. **Awareness:** Developing awareness is crucial for personal growth. This step involves becoming more mindful of your thoughts, emotions, and behaviors. By being aware of these aspects of yourself, you can better understand why you do what you do and make more conscious choices.

3. **Imagination:** Imagination is the fuel for creativity and innovation. This step encourages individuals to tap into their imagination to envision their ideal life, goals, and aspirations. It's about dreaming big and believing that anything is possible.

4. **Nurture:** Self-care and self-love are essential components of personal growth. This step emphasizes the importance of nurturing yourself—physically, emotionally, mentally, and spiritually. It could involve practicing self-care activities, setting boundaries, and prioritizing your well-being.

5. **Beliefs:** Our beliefs shape our reality. This step involves examining and challenging limiting beliefs that may be holding you back. By replacing negative beliefs with empowering ones, you can change your mindset and achieve optimal success and fulfillment.

6. **Optimism:** Cultivating gratitude and a positive mindset is critical to overcoming obstacles and staying resilient in the face of challenges. This step encourages individuals to adopt a hopeful outlook on life and focus on possibilities rather than limitations.

7. **Wins:** Celebrating victories, no matter how small, is essential for building confidence and momentum. This step involves acknowledging your achievements and milestones along the way, which can motivate you to keep moving forward on your journey of self-discovery and empowerment.

By embracing these principles in the R.A.I.N.B.O.W. framework, individuals can indeed unlock their potential, overcome obstacles, and live their best lives. This holistic approach addresses various aspects of personal growth and empowers individuals to create meaningful change in their lives.

Surprisingly, I came to view cancer as a "New Beginning" that guided me toward my true purpose in life. Life, once seen as fragile, now appeared beautiful and priceless.

In my journey of self-development, I've achieved significant milestones, including becoming a Certified PGI Consultant and a Certified Napoleon Hill Institute Certified Global Coach. These certifications signify my commitment to personal and professional growth, as well as my dedication to guiding others on their paths to success.

Through rigorous training and examination, I have honed my expertise in personal development strategies with the Proctor Gallagher Institute (PGI) and coaching methodologies rooted in Napoleon Hill's principles of success. I am passionate about empowering individuals to unlock their full potential and achieve their goals. I am committed to continuing my journey of learning and development to serve others better.

As a transformational life coach, becoming a certified facilitator of integrative and complementary practices for holistic well-being, I developed a powerful approach to support the healing process in my clients. My combined expertise in mindset principles and energy medicine positioned me as a guide who could facilitate healing on multiple levels.

My holistic approach went beyond traditional methods. It recognized the interconnectedness of the spirit, mind, and body. Through my guidance, individuals embarked on a path of self-discovery and transformation. With a deep understanding of the spirit-mind-body connection, I equipped my clients with the tools and practices needed to navigate their personal journeys, enabling them to create a life filled with joy, purpose, and inner harmony.

As I stand at this moment, reflecting on the journey that has led me here, I am filled with a profound sense of gratitude and accomplishment. Over the past two decades, I have poured my heart and soul into empowering individuals through education and guidance. As the CEO/Founder of Bounce Back for Life and Sparking Change Now, I have had the privilege of touching lives across the globe, helping others connect with their authentic selves and navigate their paths toward personal and professional success.

My book, "The Power of the Rainbow: Seven Steps to Spark Change in YOU," has been a labor of love. It unveils the transformative R.A.I.N.B.O.W. framework that has inspired countless individuals to take control of their destinies. Through my work as an author, educator, and inspirational speaker, I have witnessed the incredible power of personal growth and transformation.

Hosting "Sparking Change with Gigi" on e360tv has been a highlight of my career. It allows me to share the stories of remarkable individuals who have overcome adversity and embraced change. Through their stories, I hope to ignite a spark of motivation in others, encouraging them to embark on their own journey of self-discovery and empowerment.

As I continue this path, I am humbled by the opportunity to make a difference in the lives of others. My work is not just a profession—it is my passion, my purpose, and my calling.

Message for my friends across the globe:

I invite you to join me on this journey of growth, possibility, and endless potential. Drawing from my personal experience, I believe that individuals can unlock their potential and overcome obstacles by embracing the principles in the R.A.I.N.B.O.W. framework. This holistic approach addresses various aspects of personal growth and empowers individuals to create meaningful change in their lives.

Golden Nugget

"Listen To Your Soul and Discovery Your Truth"

About Author:

Name – Giovanna Tartarone
Contact – https://sparkingchangenow.com

Giovanna Tartarone is the CEO and founder of Rainbow Alternative Healing and Bounce Back for Life Coaching. She has been dedicated to coaching and guiding her clients to discover their full potential, helping them lead healthier, happier, and more fulfilling lives.

Chapter 4

Cindy Edington

The Long Road to Discovering "Me"

My name is Cindy Edington. I am from Fairport, NY, USA, and I am the owner of Tranquil Heart Wellness. I am a Certified Transformational Life Coach, Yoga Therapist, Reiki Master Teacher, and EFT Practitioner.

I specialize in helping women navigate the aftermath of divorce, guiding them to rise from the challenges with newfound strength. Having experienced a heart-breaking divorce myself, I understand the struggles with self-blame, financial worries, being a single mom, and anxieties about dating again. My mission is to assist women in finding their inner grounding, re-igniting their passion for life, and embracing their unique power, all while renewing their hearts to love themselves fully. My deepest desire and wish is to help as many women as I can move through these challenges faster and with greater ease to start living their best lives now.

Before I begin, let me preface that my story comes from a "healed" place. I no longer carry hurt, anger, or feel wounded by certain events, and I am not here to blame or shame anyone. I am simply sharing situations as I perceived them, how they affected me, and how I grew from them. My journey involves a past of survival, a present of self-actualization, and a hopeful future of transcendence.

Okay, let's start at the beginning...I grew up in the outer suburbs of Buffalo, NY, and I come from very humble beginnings. I am the eldest of three children, and I have two younger brothers. My father was a law enforcement officer, and my mom was a stay-at-home mom until I was 13 when she went back to work as a bank teller.

My parents had the typical "50's" style marriage. My father was the head of the house, the "breadwinner," and whatever he said ruled. Because of my father's position, there was always a lot of pressure to do the right thing and learn how to do things quickly, which meant that he was only going to show you something once. You better not make any mistakes, be perfect and up to his standards, so that you do not reflect poorly on him.

To stay in my father's good favor, I became the harmonizer in the family—the people-pleaser. My mom was the nurturer in the family unit. She took care of everything to run the household and raise us kids—even when she went back to work. My parents worked very hard for everything they got. Money was tight, and there was a lot of negative messaging around people who had money.

We also moved quite a few times throughout my childhood. I found it difficult, as each time, I was bullied quite a bit by other kids. I always felt like I had to change who I was to fit in. So, I became a chameleon, changing my colors to fit into the crowd I was with or the crowd I wanted to be a part of.

I was the first in our family to graduate from college, albeit a two-year program. My mom was a big influence and encourager of going to college. She told me, "You need an education so you can take care of yourself and not depend on a man." These were very insightful words that I didn't realize at the time, but they would also be prophetic.

By the way, I went back to college to advance my education when I was 40. My father, on the other hand, thought I would get married, and my husband would take care of me. At the time, I really wanted to go to school to be a medical examiner and support criminal investigations. I wanted to be like Quincy on the TV show! Those dreams and others I had were dashed when my parents would point out how much money it was going to cost, how it was a bad idea, and all of the possible ways that I could fail.

So, I learned very early on how to survive. I learned all the things necessary to feel safe and to be a success, although I was not aware of any of this at the time. I was driven by circumstances and the messages I had received. These messages carried over into my personal and professional adult life.

Some of my greatest assets have been my ability to get along well with others, my flexibility, and my ability to quickly adapt to new situations. These qualities gave me the capacity to establish rapport and build good relationships with people at all levels, and they helped me grow and expand into many different roles.

I spent 35 years working in research and development in Infectious Disease, Ophthalmology, Oncology, and Neurology. Because of my ability to be a chameleon, I was able to shift into various roles over the years, including roles as a bench scientist, working in clinical research operations, project and program management, account management, business development, and consulting.

Even though I was considered a success in my professional life, there came a point in time when the negative aspects of my early messaging came to the forefront. These negative aspects revealed themselves as I was growing and developing in my self-discovery. I started to notice how often I gave away my personal power, especially to men who were in positions of power. I saw how the early messages I had received regarding the ways I could fail kept me playing small.

The story of who I am today and who I am still becoming started with a heart-opening event. As I mentioned before, I went through a heart-breaking divorce years ago that left me feeling broken, unworthy, and not good enough. I was scared, alone with a baby, and had very little support. At the same time, with that heartbreak came great gifts. The gift of self-discovery, personal growth, and discovering my purpose and passion work. So many lessons, or shall I say opportunities for growth, were presented along the way and continue to be presented.

Where to begin? My ex and I were together for almost nine years. We dated for a time, moved in together, bought a house, and then got married. As my ex was five years older than me, when he turned 35, he started getting worried about being too old to start a family.

So, we decided to try to get pregnant. Sadly, it took about a year. And, the weekend I found out I was pregnant was the weekend he told me he didn't want to be married anymore, with no explanation except to say, "It wasn't me."

When I went home to tell my parents what was going on, my father asked me, "What did you do?" I was utterly taken aback by his question and thought, oh my gosh, how is this my fault? My ex had been seeing someone on the side, and yet somehow this was my fault?!

This one question had a significant impact on my subconscious, and I went into super perfectionism mode. I started to question my worth, and my self-talk reel kept saying I should have been prettier, more intelligent, a better wife, etc. In other words,

I blamed myself. On a subconscious level, a limiting belief came to the surface: You are not lovable unless you are perfect.

My ex left me with lots of debt and very little financial support for our infant daughter. I remember times when I had $10 to my name after paying all the bills and taking care of my daughter's needs. I lived on carrots, apples, and yogurt, vowing that some-day I would never go hungry again. You would think I would have gone to my parents for help, but I didn't. I was too proud and felt that if I did, then I would confirm to my father that I was not good enough and that I was not strong enough to do it on my own. I was taught vulnerability was weakness, and there was no way I was going to be seen as weak!

With so few resources, I had to get very resourceful. Since I loved going to the gym to work out, my solution was to get cer-tified as a fitness instructor. It was a win-win-win. It gave me a free gym membership, extra money in my pocket, and a way to manage the stress of working full-time and being a single mom.

It was at the gym where I met my current husband. He was my aerobics instructor, and we initially met while I was preg-nant with my daughter. When he found out that I was getting divorced, he started talking to me after every class. All of my friends kept telling me, "He is so into you."

I really didn't believe it because, again, my negative self-talk was saying, "Who wants to date someone with a baby?" And not for nothing; at that time, I really didn't trust men. I felt I didn't need anyone, as I had my daughter to give all my love to.

However, my husband was very persistent in his efforts, and we started with a group date. He was extremely sensitive to my situation and gave me the space I needed. When I felt he was someone I wanted to get serious with, I introduced him to my parents.

My father disapproved of him; however, rather than do what I always did to make my father happy, I said no and moved forward in the relationship with my husband. It was the first time I set a firm boundary with my father for myself without feeling guilty about it. It was the beginning of really discovering who I was and taking back my power, and it felt good.

As time passed, I moved in with my husband, and we started to build a life together. However, I struggled with letting him totally in. I had built up a hefty and almost impenetrable suit of armor. I was so afraid of going through what I went through with my ex that it cut off my ability to let my guard down.

I remained in survival mode, and it was costing me the ability to have the intimate relationship I truly wanted. Again, my husband was very sensitive to what I needed and patient. I do not understand how he stayed in it with me because I felt that I was pushing him away in so many ways.

It took me 15 years and couples' therapy before I would fully commit to marriage. I had been in survival mode for so long that I did not know how to shift into my feminine energy and fully trust not only him but also myself. *And I still struggle today with being fully in my feminine energy. But I do not judge myself for it. I see it as yet another growth opportunity. There is always more to learn, right?!*

I knew I wanted more, and the Universe answered. A colleague introduced me to yoga. As I walked out of the first class, I felt like I was walking on air. I had never felt so calm and serene within myself. It was a huge "aha" moment for me. I realized how much I relied on external validation to feel whole. It was the first time I knew from deep inside of me that I needed to get quiet and go within. It was the beginning of the deep inner work that needed to be done.

As my yoga practice deepened, so did my personal evolution and my connection to Source. I felt empowered and passionate about continuing to grow. My yoga journey led me to teach yoga and yoga therapy. I became certified in yoga therapy and have been teaching yoga for 25 years.

During my yoga therapy training, I had a huge breakthrough moment when one of the teachers did a session on yoga for grief relief. At the end of the session, I collapsed on the floor crying. It felt like he pierced my heart. I ended up hiring him as my therapist to help me through the complexities of experiencing the loss of self.

Through his support, I realized that I was a master at tucking away my feelings and that I had so much grief inside that needed to come out. His big message to me was to sit in my sadness and allow myself to feel my feelings and that my feelings were valid. Again, the early and layered messaging was coming to the forefront.

I was taught that crying was weak and not to show anger. I spent three years in therapy working through the early messages I had received from my father and all the hurt and angry feelings I had tucked in from the divorce. All this new awareness, combined with my continued yoga practice, prepared me for the next pivotal moment.

After 19 years of working at a day job that I absolutely loved, the company moved our jobs to the NYC area. I was not able to make that move, so I went back to school. However, this time, I went back for life coaching. All my colleagues encouraged me to do this since I was the person they would come to when they had issues. I gave them a safe, non-judgmental space to process.

After I graduated from CoachU, I started a coaching practice as a side hustle. In addition, I was still teaching fitness and yoga classes. I felt coaching was my true passion, and I desperately wanted to move into being a coach full-time. However, the old messages came right back up to the surface.

I had a colossal scarcity mindset block that got in the way. I felt it would be selfish and irresponsible of me, and on some level, it meant that I wasn't a good mom. I was committed to making sure my daughter was well taken care of. Even though we were living with my now-husband, I didn't trust the financial picture, and since we were not yet married, I couldn't take the risk. So, I went on into a new full-time day job.

Over the next several years, I moved through four more full-time day jobs. At the same time, I continued educating myself in the health and wellness arena. I completed restorative yoga training and chakra training and started my Reiki journey.

Reiki came to me from a restorative yoga session that I had with a cancer survivor client. While she was in her restorative poses, I would send her love and light with my hands. Little did I know that it was connected to Source energy.

At the end of the session, my client asked if I was sending her energy. I couldn't believe how strong the energy connection between us was. After that experience, Reiki just kept coming up. I started to see Reiki everywhere. I saw and felt it as a clear sign from the Universe to bring Reiki more formally into my life and my practice. I completed my Reiki Master Teacher training in 2020, and I practice some form of Reiki every day.

Continuing ...It wasn't until I turned 60 that I felt I could finally drop the day job and jump into my passion work full-time. I was no longer worried about meeting my daughter's needs. She was married and doing very well on her own. I also felt I had put enough money away to be okay. Plus, my husband agreed to keep working full-time until I turned 65—which is this year! Yes, it took me over 25 years of self-discovery work to get to this point, and my husband provided me with lots of reassurance.

When I started my full-time business, I thought the focus would be on yoga therapy. However, COVID-19 hit, and I had to pivot. Since coaching could be done by phone or virtually, I decided to buff up my coaching skills.

I entered another coaching program where I was introduced to the Emotional Freedom Technique and how it can be used to release limiting beliefs. It was a complete game-changer! I spent an entire year doing intense inner work with this technique. I was able to see all my programming – all the generational, cultural, societal, and institutional programming that had affected me, and how to release it. I recognized how gratitude, forgiveness, and compassion have been the cornerstone practices that have helped me grow and helped me move through my life's challenges, and how they continue to do so.

So, where am I today?

First and foremost, I'm married to a wonderful man and growing in our relationship. I have a beautiful daughter, a fantastic son-in-law, and two beautiful grandchildren.

I continue to learn and practice loving myself fully, flaws and all. Each step I take brings me closer to my authentic self, closer to others, and closer to Source. I know that we are all connected beings of love and light and that each of us is on a unique path to learn the lessons that we need to transform and transcend into our best selves.

Finally, I'm doing the work I love—sharing all that I have learned with other women to help them start living their best lives now! Life is good....... and I look forward to what comes next.

Golden Nugget

"When one door closes, trust and have faith that a new door is waiting for you to walk through and into a brighter future!"

About Author:
Name – Cindy Edington
Contact – https://tranquilheartwellness.com/

My name is Cindy Edington, a Transformational Life Coach, Certified Yoga Therapist, Reiki Master Teacher, and EFT Practitioner. I help women navigate the aftermath of divorce, guiding them to rise with newfound strength. Having experienced a heart-breaking divorce, I understand the struggles of self-blame, financial worries, single motherhood, and dating anxieties. My mission is to assist women in finding their inner grounding, reigniting their passion for life, and embracing personal power. My deepest desire is to help women move through these challenges faster and with greater ease so they can start living their best lives now.

Chapter 5

Jennifer Rogers
Rise of a Phoenix

"No, no, no, please don't let him be home," she thought to herself as she came through the alley from school, catching a glimpse of her house. But somehow, she knew. She could feel it that day. The car was gone, but it was "he" who was home. A strange pull began to flow in her small eight-year-old body, a feeling she had never felt before. A feeling she did not understand, did not yet have a name for but was not scared of. Instead, she embraced this newfound rush of energy and, with the pounding of her heartbeat, matched her steps to the beat, gripped the worn straps of her oversized backpack, and turned the other way. That day, she was not going home. That day was enough. That day, she would say no. That day, she would make her own way. That day, she set the trajectory of her destiny. That day, a Phoenix that lay dormant inside her began to awaken.

Where it began:

Sunday, August 31, 1980, a three-pound five oz baby girl was delivered six weeks early to teenage parents. Her mother, having just celebrated her 16th birthday three weeks earlier, and her father, a 19-year-old still trying to define himself, are now facing the devastating news that their baby has not survived delivery. With their world crumbling down around them in the delivery room, a team of nurses worked steadfastly to pump life into this tiny soul. Mirroring the eruption of Mount St. Helens just three months earlier, through the beeps, squeals, and pulsating sounds of the vital machines, she lets out an igneous scream and takes her first breath. She signifies her arrival into this life. This Phoenix truly is being born through chaos and ashes.

For the first few years of my life, I would surmise that it would be "normal" if there were such a thing. I do not have many memories before age four, so it seems it must have been pretty uneventful-unless you count that time at three years old, I needed to go to the bathroom so badly, I jumped out of my dad's moving car.

Yes! A moving car down a dirty gravel road as we rounded a curve, crossing a bridge heading to get my mom from work. Clearly, car seat safety was not as important then, nor was the invention of a child safety lock. Miraculously, I limped away with only scrapes of elbows, knees, and a bloody nose.

Today, at 43 years old, I still bear a scar under my nose, showing my only genuine injury. Looking back, it seems this accident was preparing me, showing others how strong I would be in life, a willingness to stand up for myself, and refusing to take "No, you can wait."

As some young marriages do, my parents did not last, and they were divorced by the time I was three. Each of them, still young, resolved to move back in with their parents. Following the divorce, my brother and I lived with our mom but spent what time we could with our dad. I was especially fond of my dad and, until his death, would sit on his lap where he would ask me, "Who's girl are ya? You're daddy's girl, huh!" I remember the warmth of his hugs, the strength of his arms around me, and the safety I felt when with him. How lucky was I that David Harold Edwards was MY daddy?

He proved one night just how strong those arms were and earned the title of being my hero. One of the memories I recall vividly was during a stay with him and my grandparents. In the early morning hours, our home caught fire.

The hot water tank exploded, and within minutes, the small trailer home was engulfed and capsulated in red-hot flames. My dad carried my brother and me out and placed us in a car. He and my grandfather then re-entered the home and carried my grandmother out. There remained one inside, my paternal great-grandmother, Bessie.

My dad and grandfather tried again and again to go back into the home to save her, but the flames and heat made it impossible. From the back seat of this car, I stood watching red and orange flames raging from every direction of the home. And for the first time, I saw an angel. I see her as clear today as I did that early morning, an angel with my great-grandmother, Bessie, floating away from the home.

At three years old, I should have been screaming and frantic, but I recall the calmness and peace I felt when witnessing this. I remember telling my mom about seeing this angel. But who believes a three-year-old? I do not remember telling my dad, but I knew he always carried the guilt and shame of having not been able to go back into the home just one more time.

Maybe that is why I never told him. His mother's (my grandmother's) body, from that day on, bore scars of that fire. But, more importantly, they served as a reminder of the time her husband and son, my DADDY, saved her.

This back-and-forth between our parents continued for a few years. At some point, my mom met someone who would become her second husband. To this day, how and where is unknown to me; the best I can fathom is that she must have been hanging out in Hell.

Mom, my brother, and I moved away from our family and onto this farmland owned by his family. We were hours away from our grandparents, our cousins, our dad, and what would become most important, those who could protect us. We moved into a trailer home he lived in with his cousin/cousins and, depending on the night, any number of their children. My brother and I were now sharing a bedroom and sleeping in one bed with another child we had just met.

That child was the youngest, so it was arranged that he would sleep by the wall, my brother, just over a year old, in the middle, and myself on the edge by the door. Gross, having to share a bed with two diaper-assed, piss-pot boys; what girl wanted that?! Certainly not me!!

Looking back, fear is not my first memory or emotion in this new place. It was listening to as loud as I could, learning the words to, and singing along with the 1984 hit by Sammy Hagar, "I Can't Drive 55." Imagine that four-year-old Jennifer subconsciously dreaming of getting away. That song was fast, fun, adventurous, catchy, and not at all like the dark of the night that was about to introduce itself slowly, fearfully, meticulously, and calculated.

The first time I saw the shadow of someone sitting on the edge of the bed, the heaviness of their hand between my tiny legs touching me, my eyes didn't need rubbing to wake up or light to see. They were opened wide, my heart racing, and with a clear voice, I asked, "What are you doing?"

The reply? "Oh, I was checking to see if you needed to use the bathroom." I knew immediately something was wrong, but at four years old, you do not know what and certainly did not argue with adults. The shadow of that person never entered my room again. In my young mind, I rationalized maybe he was telling the truth and really checking on me about the bathroom. So, I said nothing to my mom.

I did, however, say something to one of my new girl cousins. She was more than familiar with him and was strangely excited. She explained that he, too, came to her and shared more of the things he does and was surprised I did not want him to do the same to me. I remember thinking this was weird; no one in my family did these things—or, at least, that I knew about yet.

This shadow and the man it belonged to draped on me a new fabric of doubt and worry that seeped into the fibers that are still woven into me today. I absolutely hate and will not sleep on the side of the bed closest to the door. Thanks, asshole, for blocking my quickest exit in an emergency!

Soon, we moved off that farm and into town a few miles away. This was a new and exciting start. Our house was a huge two-story! With all the living space downstairs and three bedrooms upstairs, my brother and I finally had our own rooms. We were each at opposite ends of the hallway, with his being closest to the top of the stairs, our moms in the middle, and mine at the end of the hallway. We had a yard; we had neighbors and kids to play with. The school was only six blocks or so away, and I was often allowed to ride my Strawberry Shortcake bike there and back. This felt like home, like family, for a while.

Unlike the shadow of the man on the farm, I cannot recall the first time he came into my room. But I can recall the pressure of his hand across my mouth, the stench of his cigarette breath and stained teeth, the scratchy feeling of his beard, and the cold tone in his words as the threats poured off his split tongue like snake's venom. Threatening to bite and strike me if I made a move, made a sound, or told anyone. While he lay there among us, curled up, camouflaged, cold-blooded, waiting for each opportunity to slither once more into my bedroom.

The visits became more frequent. All the threats you can imagine and those you possibly could not, he said into my ears with a whisper louder than a scream I have ever heard. How could I stop this? I do not want him to hurt me and my family. I want to live; I want them to live. I do not like this; it hurts, and it is wrong. I know it is.

What do I do? What can I do? I know, or I thought I would have my brother sleep with me. After my mom went to bed, I snuck down the hall to get my brother out of his bed and have him come to my room.

Hoping and praying this would deter him, it seemed as if it only made the challenge of this sickness more fun. Once I started bringing my brother to my room, a hook lock appeared on the outside of the door of my mom's room. He had now begun locking her in the room at night while in my room.

Great! I thought, surely, she would wake up, he would not be in bed, and she would not be able to leave the room. He will have to say what he was doing. Yes, my mom will stop this! That would have been too easy; that story of rescue never happened.

At some point, I stopped getting my brother from his bed and moved to lining up toys from the entrance of my door to the edge of my bed. Now, I could wake myself up when he entered my room instead of a hand on my face. In the morning, I would put away the toys, make my bed, ride my bike to school, and go through my day as if these terrible things were not happening to me in the night.

My room was spotless as a child, and there was nothing out of place because this was the one thing I could control. But I opened my closet; it was a different world. A world of mess of piled clothes, clean mixed with dirty, a constant battle I fought silently within myself, school papers tossed about instead of hung proudly, and blankets used as forts to escape to a different world. No light was allowed in this closet because I could enter, shut the door, be alone, and escape the nightmare that was happening just on the other side.

The day came when my body nor that closet would let me hide those whispers any longer. An infection had taken over, and the pain was intolerable. I was now eight years old, and for the first time in three years, the secrets of my nights had to reveal themselves. Stepping down the squeaky stairs, one foot in front of the other, I called out to my mom and said to her what had been happening. Begging and pleading with her not to say anything, she took me next door to our neighbors to use their phone.

When the police arrive at our home, I'm immediately asked to repeat my story and taken to the hospital. In a freezing, bright, white, and sterile room, lying on a bed, my clothes are cut from my body. Today, I can still feel the coldness of those scissors as they glided along my leg, cutting my pants, and the crunching sound the material made as it separated into two pieces. I can still feel the heat of the tears as they streamed down my face as strange people asked me again what happened, examined me, and then confirmed to my mom my truth.

Now, she was forced to face what was happening to her daughter, but what was she to do? The man doing this was the same man she relied on for shelter, support, financial security, and, truth be told, love. She packed the two-story home with all their belongings and moved to a small two-bedroom home a block away from the school. But if you think he stayed behind, you are wrong. And if you think the abuse stopped, well, we are all wrong.

My days looked different after we moved to the smaller house. My brother and I went back to sharing a bedroom, and instead of a bed, we now slept on a small couch. I no longer had a closet to hide in, and my secrets were out. Somewhere along the way, my Strawberry Shortcake bike was broken, and now I walked the short distance to school. Instead of entering my bedroom at night, he would now wait until I was home alone and watch me bathe, telling me which parts of my small body to wash or touch as he sat on the toilet like a hawk eyeing its prey. All the while, I am still waiting for the police or someone, anyone, to help.

One afternoon, when I came home from school, I saw that our car had gone from our home. "No, no, no, please don't let him be home," I thought to myself. But I knew. I could feel it through my core that day. The car was gone, but it was he who was home. A strange pull began to flow in my small body, a feeling I had never felt before. A feeling I did not understand, did not yet have a name for but was not scared of.

59

Instead, I embraced this newfound rush of energy and, with the pounding of my heartbeat, matched my steps to the beat, gripped the worn straps of my oversized backpack, and turned the other way. That day, I was not going home. That day, I had enough. That day, I was saying no.

I walked a mile and a half outside of town to my mom's friend Tina's home and knocked on the door. Surprised to see me standing on her porch, she asked, "Jennifer, what are you doing here?" and led me inside. There, sitting on her dining room floor as we placed potting soil and seeds into small Styrofoam cups, I shared my pain once more and asked her to please call my grandmother. She did. Tina never asked any questions; she guided me as to how to keep planting. This time felt warm to me; my grandmother was on her way. I just needed to wait a few more hours.

As we talked and lined up soiled-filled cups around the floor, a knock came on the door. Tina swooped me and my backpack up in her arms, carried me to her bedroom closet, and placed me inside. Here, she told me, "Shh, don't say anything, and stay right here; be very quiet." From the dark floor of her closet, I could hear her make her way to the front door and open it.

It was my mom. From the sound of her voice, she was crying. I heard her say, "I can't find Jennifer. We don't know where she is. She was at school today, but she never made it home." At that moment, hearing the trembling and concern in my mom's voice, I was immediately torn on the inside. I didn't know what to do; I didn't mean to hurt my mom.

Scared and shaking myself, I then heard Tina say with a calmness and confidence I had never heard in a woman's voice, "Dottie, I have Jennifer, and you are not getting her back." And just like that, all the confusion, anxiousness, doubt, and trepidation I had left my body like a bolt of lightning. For the first time, I felt someone stand up for me, someone believe in me, someone listen to me. For the first time since meeting "him," I felt safe.

Many times over my life, I have looked back and thanked that little eight-year-old girl for the strength and courage she carried that day. I have called on her in times of darkness and loneliness and asked for her guidance to help lead me through. Each time I find myself living in a moment of doubt, I am reminded of this specific day, as if it happened yesterday and not 35-plus years ago.

She reminds me just how strong I really am simply by placing one foot in front of the other and taking that next step. While this is not the end of my story or the traumas I would go on to experience, it was the birthplace of the woman I would grow to become, the woman I am today. The Phoenix I arose to. I invite you to connect with me to see how we can rise together.

Golden Nugget

"I am pure magic!"

About Author:
Name – Jennifer Rogers
Contact – https://www.facebook.com/jennifer.glover.5

A generational trauma breaker with a passion for empowering women. As a survivor of childhood abuse, I've risen from adversity, earning a bachelor's degree in human resources, leading teams for over 17 years, and now serving as the Client Services Director at Apela Strategic Solutions. My heart's work is coaching and empowering women, fostering growth and confidence through life's challenges, and providing a safe space for them to rise like the Phoenix from their own trials.

Chapter 6

Anjana Lala

From People-Pleaser to Self-Love:
Anjana's Journey of Unbecoming

Meet our radiant soul, a beacon of resilience and joy, Anjana Lala, a woman who has turned life's challenges into a symphony of self-discovery. In the rich tapestry of her Hindu culture, she navigated the expectations of being the perfect people-pleasing daughter, wife, and daughter-in-law.

Burden of Niceness

Bless my mother, who wanted to protect her daughter by empowering her with the skills to be the perfect girl, daughter, wife, and daughter-in-law. She was doing her best with her level of understanding at the time in a culture where it was the norm.

However, this relentless pursuit of perfection came at a devastating cost: it suppressed my individuality and robbed me of my voice. My body, mind, and spirit cried. It would not accept this suppression of my being. My intuition was sharp and expressed itself as sensitivity and softness. But this was not cool for my caregivers.

Constantly bombarded with messages about my "excessive sensitivity" and tearful nature, I was bombarded with phrases like "stop being a crybaby" and "wear your big girl panties." These pronouncements served only to belittle my powerful and passionate emotions, framing them as an unwelcome inconvenience incompatible with the role I was expected to be and play.

The message was clear: my primary purpose was to ensure everyone's happiness and maintain a facade of unruffled peace. My innocent heart and my being were not welcome into the world I was born into. Thus began my transformation into a human Swiss Army Knife—a fixer, an overgiver, and a chronic people-pleaser. My life became an endless cycle of revolving around other people's problems, approval, and needs, dictating my every move. Now, I was regarded as a good girl, a nice girl, and a reliable daughter. A school exercise greatly emphasized this fierce niceness.

The Masks We Wear:

A school exercise where classmates described each other so-lidified this reality. Over 95 percent of the comments echoed the same sentiment: "She's very nice, always helpful, and always available." This pattern repeated itself in countless team-building sessions at my corporate jobs, with the label of "the ever-re-liable nice helper" clinging to me like a second skin.

However, beneath this facade of unrelenting niceness festered a pit of misery. I felt hollowed out, adrift in a sea of emptiness, numb to the world around me. My life was a bitter pill I was forced to swallow, the sweetness of existence replaced by a constant undercurrent of frustration, resentment, and an over-whelming urge to please. It's not that I want their approval, but I need their approval.

My entire life became a whirlwind of trying, crying, and strug-gling to be enough and do enough. And yet, not too much. People pleasers like me know the agony that comes from yearning to be liked and yielding to almost anything or anyone. But there is always anxiety lingering: What if they see through my mask? What if they find my flaws, scars, and bruises? What if they discover my most authentic, deepest self and reject me?

People-pleasing can be tiresome. This constant push-and-pull between wanting to be liked but fiercely keeping every-one at arm's length conflicts with my heart, longing for deep, genuine connection, and the mask protecting my vulnerable parts. Vulnerability isn't for everyone or universal. You see, people-pleasing keeps you forever in the shackles of comfort, which leads to conformity. Conformity is like wearing clear lip balm. Everyone wears it.

This relentless cycle inevitably led to the same devastating outcome – me, isolated, lonely, and consumed by a suffocating sense of self-loathing.

The most crippling consequence of my people-pleasing tendencies was a profound sense f self-estrangement. I had no idea who I indeed was, what I desired, or what truly brought me joy.

The concept of meaningful connection with others was lost on me. I had become an expert at mirroring others, morphing into whatever I perceived would gain their approval. It was easier to navigate life this way. This relentless self-denial manifested in a brutal inner critic who relentlessly labeled me as "fat, ugly, boring, stupid, a coward, a misfit, and utterly insignificant."

I also grappled with an identity obscured by conformity. The darkness of this left a life unlived in my teens and 20s when I witnessed people of my age having fun and taking risks. My heart yearned for those experiences: traveling, taking chances, dating, trying new things, having groups of friends, and going on adventures.

I was stuck in my fear of living—yes, fear of living. All the "what ifs" consumed my mind: What if they judged me? What if I looked like a fool? What if I couldn't do it? What if they didn't like me? What if they laughed at me? The what-ifs stopped me from exploring who I was or could be.

Yet, I remember my teachers and corporate managers always stating that I was intelligent and had a lot of potential. In my mind, that was just utter nonsense. I don't know what they are seeing me. I had no reflection on this. (In the corner of my heart, I hoped it would come true.) This attention caused such anxiety and feeling that I was not good enough so profoundly. I did not understand why I didn't feel good enough. It deepened the feeling of not belonging, inadequacy, loneliness, and unworthy of love—a life of dissatisfaction and discontent.

The regrets of letting go of all opportunity's life presented to me. Just deciding to explore the opportunity was painful. Deciding, for me, was a lengthy, anxious, and highly stressful experience.

I remember, for example, being one of the few students chosen for a Computer Science course when I was in school. Computer programming just became a thing, and my school selected me for this. I distinctly recall feeling scared and anxious when I was called into the principal's office.

What did I do wrong? What am I going to be blamed for? They shared the good news, yet I was not excited about it. Instead, I feel a sinking feeling in the pit of my tummy. The other students were so thrilled and could not wait to tell their parents.

What did I do? I kept quiet, did not tell anyone, and just said no. To protect myself against being judged, I did not attend this course. My teachers asked me so many times if I was sure, and my answer was always NO.

Later in the year, I asked my friend, who was also selected, how it was going. She gave me the details. A deep sense of disappointment and sorrow washed over me. My body was cold, and tears gushed down my eyes—a spontaneous reaction by my body, mind, and heart.

These buried emotions and suppressed opinions created low self-worth and value, which I hid from the world by wearing the mask of a very friendly, happy, "NICE" girl.

The Turning Point

A personal pivotal moment arrived in 1997 when fate intervened. My brother, unable to attend a seminar on mind power, offered me his spot. Hesitantly, I entered the world of John Kihoe and his book, and it was a revelation. The scales fell from my eyes, exposing the true nature of my chronic people-pleasing behavior and its impact on my life of not being good enough.

I found a way to feel good about myself. I am smiling. I am happy. It fills my heart with mushiness when I think about this every time—that yummy feeling of tears, laughter, and relief. I could breathe and only understood how I choked my vitality by being too nice for too long. This newfound awareness ignited a fire within me—a burning desire to rewrite my own story, discover who I wanted to be and carve a path toward a life of fulfillment and meaning. I went on adventures, small and big.

Shedding the Armor:

One seemingly ordinary day at a restaurant, waiting for a friend who was perpetually late – no call, no text, just another instance of being taken for granted – became a turning point. The familiar anger bubbled up, a potent cocktail of frustration and resentment. This time, however, something shifted. I reached a breaking point. The dam broke.

"Stop! Enough!" I declared, my voice surprisingly firm, perhaps even a little loud. "Can you just be on time? Is it too much to ask? I'm sick and tired of waiting for you. No more! I matter, and my time matters. Do you get that?!"

The words tumbled out in a torrent of pent-up emotion. I trembled, shocked by my audacity. A stunned silence followed, a testament to the seismic shift that had just occurred. This decisive moment, forever etched in my memory, marked my true liberation.

The relief was immense, like a breath of fresh air after years of suffocating under the weight of niceness. This suffocating "niceness" was the armor I had donned to navigate the world as a people-pleaser. Living as a chameleon for decades had left me utterly clueless about my true self and my core beliefs. A dark cloud of inadequacy and self-doubt hung over me wherever I went. My self-loathing was so pervasive it threatened to consume me whole. "Day in and day out," I confessed, "I ruminated on how unattractive, boring, and stupid I was. All I wished for was to be intelligent, pretty, and successful."

Yet, in the absence of acknowledgment and encouragement, I persevered, rising above the echoes of "not good enough" and "too much." Denied the room to explore my world simply because I was a girl, I faced rejection and emotional neglect, weaving a protective wall around my heart. The first half of my life was a blur of self-denial and fear. I hid from myself and the world. The first half of my life was a blur of hiding, fearing exposure, and trying to be everything to everyone. It was a life of invisibility and self-abandonment.

Recovery from people-pleasing was a process of self-discovery. I had to learn about boundaries, values, and what I truly wanted from work, friends, and life in general. I explored the concept of self-care and began prioritizing activities that nourished my body, mind, and spirit. Slowly, I unlearned the ingrained habits of people-pleasing and embraced my authentic self.

Unbecoming and Thriving

A momentous awakening at 40 led me to a transformative journey—a journey where I embraced Laughter Yoga, traveled solo (for the first time in my life) to India, and became a Laughter Yoga Teacher and Coach. Laughter Yoga became the catalyst that brought me back to life, awakening a sense of liberation.

Laughter Yoga helped me connect with my body, mind, and energy. It helped reduce my tightness. As I practiced Laughter Yoga daily, I released the stored tension, trauma, emotions, anger, sadness, fear, and frustration. My body became lighter, and I became less anxious and worried less about all the small things in life. My "what if" thought process slowed down.

It helped me remove one mask at a time, break the shackles of people-pleasing, and come out of my closet of invisibility. Laughter Yoga was like wearing that special red lipstick. You get washed over by something special that lights you up with vitality to live.

Laughter Yoga created calmness; calmness became courage, and courage became confidence. Confidence became catchy. Laughter is definitely the best medicine. I know it's a cliché, but damn, it's great medicine. Laughter brings with it joy and happiness.

I learned how to swim, did public speaking for the first time in front of fifty people, and facilitated a laughter workshop with 100 people for the first time. I even took a three-month contract to work in another country for the first time in my life. So many "first-time" experiences continued in that year. I now understand when they say life begins at 40...laughing with joy. Yes, I feel happy and brave. My motto from that day was and is saying YES TO LIFE.

The Ripple Effect

I, Anjana, realized the power of choice—intentional and aware. I embarked on a series of exhilarating adventures, from workshops and public speaking to a three-month contract in another country, swimming lessons, and mastering the art of riding a bicycle. Ooooh, my inner child reveled in the joy of trying new things, marking the beginning of my Unbecoming! Living Life okay, I claim it. Thriving!

Through these millions of small adventures, I unearthed my inner strength and fell deeply in love with myself. Unbecoming became the liberation from the shackles of people-pleasing and conformity, creating a ripple effect—increased self-worth, diminished fear, meaningful connections, and fulfilling work. Stepping out of my hidden closet of niceness, I changed everything and continued to learn, unbecome, and have fun. I am okay with not everyone liking me or fitting in. The most important thing is I am becoming my most authentic self.

A String of Hope

My wish is that for all the people pleasers out there, there is hope of finding your heart, your voice, and your wholeness.

You, the weaver of countless wishes, the magician of making others smile, hold power to weave a life that sings your own melody. The journey to self-discovery may feel like a tangled knot, but within you lies the strength to gently untangle it, thread by thread.

Remember, the applause of others doesn't define your worth. It's the quiet hum of your own happiness, the vibrant colors you bring to your world. It's okay to say no, to set boundaries, to let go of requests that drain your light. As you do, a space opens for your authentic voice to emerge. It might be a whisper at first, but with each honest expression, it grows stronger and clearer.

This newfound freedom won't diminish your ability to connect. It will deepen it. People crave authenticity, and the more you embrace yours, the more genuine connections you'll attract. Let your "yes" be a resounding joy and your "no" a form of self-care.

The path to flow may not be linear, but with each step of self-discovery, you'll find the rhythm of your own heart. It's in the quiet moments, the hobbies you explore, the dreams you dare to chase. Embrace the flow, the state where your passions and purpose intertwine. It's there you'll discover a life that's not just pleasing but profoundly fulfilling.

So, take a deep breath, dear people pleaser. Your voice deserves to be heard; your light deserves to shine. This is the start of a beautiful symphony composed by you, for you.

Golden Nugget

"Live life to your OWN Beat and Rhythm!"

About Author:

Name – Anjana Lala

Contact – www.anjanalala.com

Imagine waking up one morning and realizing you don't need to search for your "spirit animal" in the cereal aisle anymore. You are a powerful tigress, and you're ready to roar!

But wait...Hold on, did my brain just "MEOW"?

I am your secret weapon to an extraordinary next chapter. I'm Anjana Lala, your multi-talented Midlife Designer Coach. I guide incredible women 47+ like you navigate the jungle of hot flashes, societal aging expectations, and identity crisis dread...all with a healthy dose of humour and a giant glass of wine (optional, but highly recommended).

So, ditch the dull & doubt, stop people-pleasing and embrace the fierce. Let's channel your inner Beyonce and go on a midlife adventure.

Chapter 7

Julie A. Diaz

Rock your Health Journey!

Have you ever brought a list of issues to review with your doctor, and your doctor gave it a quick glance and then took control of the appointment without ensuring your questions were addressed? Has a doctor ever scoffed at you for searching on the internet for health information? There is nothing wrong with researching your health conditions. It would be unwise not to learn about your body and your health.

Undiagnosed

For ten years, I knew I had a thyroid problem based on my symptoms. I visited at least 12 different doctors during this time span, seeking a diagnosis. My efforts failed because my TSH (Thyroid Stimulating Hormone) test was always normal. My T3 and T4 thyroid hormone levels were also in range, although a few lab tests indicated that my T3 was on the low end of the range.

One doctor after another failed to run the test that would have revealed my diagnosis. I was usually told I was fine. A few doctors offered me Prozac and birth control pills, both of which have serious side effects, and thus I refused. They don't know this, but I fired them! It's funny they never followed up or checked on me.

I was finally referred to an endocrinologist in the tenth year after my symptoms began. At last, an abnormal test result was discovered because this doctor ran the thyroid antibody tests (TPO and TG). Twenty years ago, there was not a lot of buzz about Hashimoto's like there is now. Although I had researched, I was not familiar with these tests, and I had not considered autoimmune disease as a possibility.

I would have been in the dark even longer if I had not been able to see what the doctor was writing on my chart. I saw her writing my diagnosis, "Consistent with Hashimoto's." She wasn't going to tell me! I asked her if that was my diagnosis, and she quietly answered yes. She gave me a prescription for levothyroxine and said to come back in six months. I fired her at that moment and never returned. Do you think her office called to check on me? No, they did not.

I discovered later through my research, and several doctors told me directly that the mainstream approach to Hashimoto's disease is to tell the patient they have hypothyroidism and pre-scribe levothyroxine. It's also typical to prescribe birth control and antidepressants to help with the symptoms. My doctors told me they do this because they do not know how to treat au-toimmune disease.

Published studies state that over 90% of hypothyroidism cases in the United States are caused by Hashimoto's autoimmune disease. Some scientists estimate that 60% of people with Hashimoto's are undiagnosed. All these people have the right to know what they are afflicted with! An estimated 50 million people in the United States have autoimmune disorders that cause the immune system to attack healthy cells and tissue. If a doctor doesn't know how to treat their patient, they should refer them to someone who *can* help, such as a functional medicine doctor, an integrative physician, or a naturopath. Even a health coach like me could provide more assistance.

Hashimoto's causes a lot of suffering. People, mostly women, experience weight gain, joint pain, severe fatigue, depression, anxiety, brain fog, skin problems, hormone imbalance, hair loss, and more. Their symptoms do not simply disappear by taking Prozac and birth control pills. Undiagnosed thyroid disease can increase the risk of serious conditions such as cardiovascular disease, infertility, diabetes, and osteoporosis.

Every patient has a right to know their proper diagnosis. If you have an autoimmune condition, you have every right to know, and you *need* to know so that you can identify and address the root causes of your condition. Thyroid hormone medication is a treatment but not a cure. Prozac and birth control pills are essentially band-aids to treat the symptoms, but the disease is left untreated and continues to progress. If it were cancer or some other serious condition, many lives would be lost. Getting diagnosed earlier would prevent a lot of suffering and save patients time and money.

Once I knew what I was dealing with, I jumped into action, and I did everything I could to improve my condition. I learned from Dr. Joseph Mercola that there is a medication that has been safely used for many years to treat most autoimmune diseases and even some cancers, but it's not an "on-label" treatment, so it is seldom prescribed. I had to search for a doctor that was willing to prescribe it for me. I felt better on day one of taking it. I write about this medication in detail in my book, *Conquer Hashimoto's*.

Remission is Possible

Autoimmune disease can be reversed. I am currently in remission. I have also been out of remission during a few highly stressful times in my life. People with Hashimoto's commonly go back and forth between remission and relapse. I am certain that it would have helped me to know my diagnosis much earlier in the disease process because more complications can result over time. I have personally faced several problems over the last 20 years since I started to become ill, and I have used holistic medicine for most of these health problems.

It has been 30 years since I developed a fascination with herbal medicine and holistic healing. I have great reverence for Gaia, mother earth. Our beautiful earth provides us with countless amazing foods and plants to nourish and heal us. Combining those with advanced science has resulted in the development of many nutraceuticals that can elevate our health and treat even the most serious diseases.

After seeing my trusting mother overmedicated (and suffering side effects), I was very concerned, and I researched every medication prescribed to her and learned about the alternatives. I found great inspiration and empowerment as I learned about safe and effective natural treatments.

I have used a combination of nutrition, herbs, oils, nutraceuticals, and various treatments to cure eczema, reverse Hashimoto's autoimmune disease, shrink thyroid nodules, prevent recurring bronchitis, treat infections and viruses, and overcome gallstones without losing my gallbladder. In the last few years, I have been experimenting with scalar frequency healing and red-light therapy, with significant positive results. I always work with my mainstream medical doctors and evaluate the available treatment options. In my personal experience, I have found holistic and integrative approaches to be safer and more effective. Addressing the root causes just makes more sense. Your body has an innate ability to heal, given the proper tools and environment.

Conquer Hashimoto's Disease

In my book, *Conquer Hashimoto's, How to Achieve Remission from Autoimmune Disease, Shrink Thyroid Nodules, and Avoid Surgery*, I show you by example that you can reclaim your health and feel happy and energetic again. My book describes how I was able to shrink my thyroid nodules and conquer Hashimoto's disease by normalizing my thyroid lab numbers while also resolving fatigue, depression, anxiety, hair and skin problems, weight gain, and more.

I teach you how to identify and address root causes, which include hidden infections, toxicity, nutrient deficiencies, gut imbalance, and more. You will learn how to heal your gut, safely detox, and resolve hidden infections. You will also learn about the different types of thyroid nodules, what the risks of thyroid surgery include, and how to prevent cancer and avoid surgery.

Conquer Hashimoto's includes a thyroid nodule reduction program as well as a comprehensive guide to healing that focuses on mind, body, and spirit. You will learn about diet, iodine, gut healing, nutraceuticals, immune modulators, antiviral herbs, light therapy, frequency healing, essential oils, and much more.

Dedication

My book is dedicated to my mother, who went undiagnosed with Hashimoto's disease for decades, which likely contributed to her many health issues. I got involved and helped her to treat herself by adding superfoods and nutraceuticals to her routine. She used to say that I kept her alive. That was the biggest compliment.

I was devastated to lose her when she was 84 years old to Covid-19 in April 2020. She was a victim of negligence in a veteran's nursing home where they moved a sick woman into her room without using clean PPE (personal protective equipment) and without cleaning her room after removing the sick patient. My mother was especially vulnerable because she had recently sustained a fall and broken a rib.

This was at the beginning of the pandemic. The National Guard came in to help because the situation was so badly managed. She was grateful to one of the guardsmen for helping her eat her breakfast because she couldn't feed herself due to her injury. However, no one assisted her with lunch or dinner.

She suffered a lot, and it still breaks my heart. She was a kind and gentle lady and a loving mother and grandmother. She served our country in two branches of the military. She helped people in her career as a nursing assistant. She deserved so much better at the end of her life. So did many other senior citizens who were victimized and separated from their families and deprived of a proper funeral.

On a Mission

Please join me on a mission to help people with Hashimoto's disease get diagnosed earlier. I plan to call on medical associations in the United States to screen for thyroid antibodies early and routinely so that people are diagnosed sooner. This will give people a better chance to reverse their conditions and prevent additional complications.

When you are Facing a Diagnosis

I understand it can be overwhelming when facing symptoms or a diagnosis. That is why I want to empower women with my story and teach them how to reverse disease and take the reins when facing health challenges.

In that regard, it is very important to assemble a great team of medical professionals. I recommend trying to find integrative physicians or having a functional medicine doctor or naturopathic doctor on your team. There are benefits to having a variety of practitioners. There is so much to learn about our health, and there is so much research being published all the time. No one person can keep current with all of it, but if you are dealing with an illness, you can be your own expert!

Be sure to keep a file on yourself with all your lab work and radiology reports. You can share your labs with other doctors as needed. I have found my doctors to be very open to seeing all my lab work, regardless of which doctors ordered it.

You can also avail yourself of health coaching. It is cost-efficient and can help to guide you and save you time and money while seeking medical care.

A quality certified health coach can help you to:

- Identify your top health concerns.
- Clearly define and document your goals.
- Review your recent medical workups and give you insights.

- Suggest lab tests you can request from your doctor.
- Identify the root causes of your illness and provide solutions.
- Document a custom diet, exercise, and supplement program.
- Refer you to specialists and/or advanced holistic treatment centers.
- Coach you on lifestyle choices that can elevate your health.
- Provide resources, recipes, tools, and eBooks to assist you.
- Motivate you to stay on track and keep track of your progress.

Our mind, body, and spirit are connected, and our emotions and beliefs affect our physical health. When you get a diagnosis, it is natural to feel concerned or frightened. However, it is best to keep a positive attitude and believe that you can heal yourself. That positive self-belief will help you to make the necessary changes to improve your condition. Having a supportive health coach to encourage you helps you to stay informed, motivated, and on track during your journey to wellness.

In my book, I provide many takeaway lists including stress reduction tips, ways to avoid toxins, lab tests to ask for, parasite-killing herbs, and more. My intention is to provide as much information as possible to help people to reverse and prevent disease, and to provide encouragement and hope because remission is attainable.

There is an endless amount of information available to all of us. Regardless of your current knowledge level, you can always discover new information, products, therapies, or inventions that may just result in a huge leap in your healing journey.

Remember to love yourself enough to speak up for yourself and take good care of yourself. Knowledge is power. Loving yourself—now that is power, too! Given the proper support and information, you can rock your health journey!

Wishing you great health and happiness.

Julie A. Diaz, New Jersey, USA

Golden Nugget

"Aim to embody and demonstrate the qualities of unconditional love, compassion, and kindness. Your energy and presence can uplift those around you, which in turn uplifts you as well."

About Author:

Name – Julie A. Diaz

Contact – https://yourwellnesschampion.com/

Julie Diaz is a Board-Certified Health Coach, Technical Writer, Author, and Speaker. She was diagnosed with Hashimoto's disease in 2012 after 10 years of suffering symptoms. Once properly diagnosed, she created her own holistic regimen and successfully shrank two thyroid nodules within two months. She was able to avoid thyroid surgery and ultimately achieve remission and reclaim her energy, happiness, and productivity.

Julie is the owner of Your Wellness Champion Health Coaching. She coaches clients with hypothyroidism, autoimmune disease, and various other health conditions. Julie helps her clients uncover the root causes of their illnesses, and to try new healthy approaches to improve their overall health.

Chapter 8

Christa Rose

Live The Life You Love

THE VALUE OF TIME

If you want to know the value of one year,
ask a student who failed a course.
If you want to know the value of one month,
ask a mother who gave birth to a premature baby.
If you want to know the value of an hour,

ask the student waiting to find out if they
were accepted to their dream school.
If you want to know the value of one-hundredth of a second,
ask the athlete who placed second place in the
100 meters in the Olympics.
If you want to know the value of eternity,
ask me about writing this chapter!

I can't hear you!

I said before they found out I was born with only 10% hearing in one ear. After surgery, I went to speech-language classes until grade 8, when I was made fun of. I quit, but I secretly kept working on developing my speech until I was confident enough not to pass out if I had to give a presentation in class! One step forward!

Slippery Spring

Time went on, and after school, I got my dream job. I clearly remember leaving work from the hospital at around 7 p.m. It was well after hearing of this massive snowstorm that hit a few hours before. Ironically, it was the first day of spring. I kept thinking we should be seeing budding flowers, not searching for snow blowers! My car skated on ice, and I was hit head-on by a full-size pickup truck.

This ordinary first day of spring turned into the last day I labeled myself as being "there."

I learned how important it is not to take for granted what I used to think of as the small things in life. It's so easy to go through the day complaining, whining, and feeling resentful until you're faced with a crushing, immense reality.

I had to start learning to let go.

I loved Lori, my hairdresser. She would cut my hair, layer it, and defuse it, and it would end up looking like a fuzzy Q-tip on my head. I would pay, give her a tip with a small smile, and drive home to wash it.

The next time, I brought in a picture of a girl who had the hairstyle I wanted. The therapy session went on, and when I looked in the mirror, my Q-tip hair was back. Now, what do I do?

I felt like a hair whore! But yes, I canceled my next appointment with Lori. It was the best move I made! No more Q-tip head for me! Surround Yourself with Good People who bring out the best in you, and you can be your authentic self. Some of my true friendships are based on a solid foundation of alcohol, sarcasm, and inappropriate shenanigans.

> *"One day, all of us will get separated from each other.*
> *We will miss our conversations. Days, months, and*
> *years will pass until we rarely see each other. One day,*
> *our children will see our photos and ask, "Who are these*
> *people?" And we will smile with invisible tears and say,*
> *"It was with them that I had the best days of my life."*
> *Unknown*

I Signed Up to Be a Wife and Mother – Not a Widow and Single Parent!

It was one year, one month, and one day after my car accident when I got that call. My husband went for a blood test, and they immediately told him to go to the hospital. They admitted him and did many other tests, including a bone marrow biopsy. The doctor called us both in and said this was the saddest news he had ever given to a young couple.

Rob had a fast and aggressive form of leukemia, and he had already had it for three or four months. Two weeks after his diagnosis, he was called by the doctor at the hospital as he was starting to go unconscious. After a CAT scan, I held his hand and put my head close to his. We shared an intimate moment as he crossed from this life to the next.

A few months later, I decided to get a hamster; unfortunately, his life was cut short. My son insisted we have a funeral. We bought a small box of doughnuts, knowing this would be Waffle's coffin. He now accepted that Waffles was gone, but still reminded me of it every time we drove by a pet store. From that day on, we didn't dare buy a 10-pack of donut holes!

Puzzle Piece

About 20 years later, I became a puzzle piece. Over four years, my overall health had deteriorated. It started with seizures, muscle spasms, and falling, plummeting white blood cells. I took many trips in the ambulance and ended up in the intensive care unit too many times to count. For a short time, I started to slip into what seemed to be a catatonic state; I couldn't move or talk, although I could hear absolutely everything.

Intubation

It just became too hard, and my body checked out. My scariest memory is when I heard the mumbling of people talking about me, and then I could see them putting oxygen masks on me.

As they were intubating me, everything went black. Then it was dark, kind of like being in space. All that pain I felt slipped away as I continued in this darkness. Suddenly, my body was engulfed with a feeling of total love. There were these white, glowing light figures starting to come closer, and I felt more love.

As I basked in the glory of this feeling, I could start to see the world as we know it clearly and everyone in it. That was my turning point. I felt this pulling sensation, and then I made a choice and drifted away from the most beautiful light and love I had ever experienced because I still had to fulfill my purpose, whatever that may be. I knew this love would always be there, but I decided to return to my body.

At that moment, I felt the hard bed underneath me and a rigid, painful structure down my throat. I started slowly wiggling a finger until I heard, "She's starting to wake up!"

A flood of doctors came to me, took out the tube, and kept oxygen on me, but I still could remember the sensation of that loving feeling despite my bodily pain.

I had no sense of the time or date. This was four days after one of my most significant episodes. Was it a dream? Was it the pain meds? Was it a near-death experience? Does it matter? I don't interpret it; I just know my experience. This was just one of the many secrets I kept so that others wouldn't think my health issues were that serious.

Mystery Solved: Diagnoses

A neurologist sent my bloodwork to a place for rare diseases, and I tested positive for Anti-Gad 65. Now, normal levels are under five, but mine? Oh no, it decided to skyrocket to a whopping 250 (finding out later it was higher, approximately 450).

Now, what on earth is Anti-Gad 65? Well, it turns out it's a rare disease that robs you of GABA. Usually, we all produce Gaba, but in my diagnosis called Anti-Gad 65, I don't produce enough. It messes with your fine motor skills, making simple tasks like typing, writing, or even zipping up zippers difficult. It also messes with your brain, affecting your memory and ability to operate a phone, speak coherently, or even find the right words. It's utterly frustrating! Fear of my future took over, and I had a hard time keeping up hope.

I was given a "time frame." As my husband and I drove home, we both balled, mainly due to fear. After the initial shock, I was determined to beat this despite the odds. I started using supplements. Who would have thought eating raw garlic could boost your immune system and so much more rather than just keeping vampires away!?

People kept telling me I was strong, but to be transparent, I wasn't always. I almost gave up many times. On my way home, we went through a drive-through. When asked what I would like to order, I said, "A large coffee with two milks," and in my mind, I continued, "With a side order of a will to live." The pain almost broke me, but I held on. Sometimes, one second at a time, but I did it.

What Doesn't Kill You Makes You Stronger

What? I can think of many other ways I would love to have blessings. I mean, I thought I had a handle on life until it broke. In my experience, my greatest tragedies were my greatest gifts. These experiences have given me my soul's purpose, which is to hold hope for others. Hope is an acronym for **H**eck **O**ver **P**leasing **E**veryone to **H**old **O**n **P**ain **E**nds.

I Made a Decision That Changed My Life

What were the secrets to starting on the road to recovery? It was changing my mindset. My words, beliefs, thoughts, and behaviors all equaled my reality. That's right, I choose my reality!

This was it; I had to change it from, *I'm never going to get better* and all those thoughts about giving up to, *I'm going to heal; I'm getting better every day. This is my final choice and decision.* Once I made that decision, all other decisions were already set on the right path. I felt as if I had a voicemail that said, "I'm out of my mind; I will be back in 10 minutes!"

As I grab my coffee, I have a flashback about how many decisions I've made, good or bad, right or wrong, suntan lotion or oil, that all determined my next move, even if that meant an embarrassing sunburn.

"In every single thing you do, you're constantly making a decision that will choose a direction. Your life is a result of each choice." Unknown

My emotions became my alarm. My life was only as good as I felt it was.

That's why I use the acronym **WAIT**, which is an acronym for "**W**hat **A**m **I T**hinking?" Whenever I start feeling even a bit of depression sneaking in, I ask myself this question to check my thoughts and see if they're true or if I'm ruminating over something that happened. I consciously run through the drama and chaos that is in my mind and then challenge myself to ask, "What do I *want* to think and feel instead?"

Self-Talk

What do you secretly say to yourselves during a day, month, or lifetime? Some for me were: "I'm so stupid; I should have left earlier; I knew this was rush hour," I said as I flew in for my appointment with my life coach, and I hate being late! "At least I remembered to bring that picture you asked me to." Even though I had no idea why, I just followed instructions. Then, she had a challenge for me.

It was to say, out loud, everything I secretly said to myself in my mind. That was easy! I didn't even have to think about it. "I let my body go, I'm a slob, my hair is frizzy..."

She stopped me there. She put a chair right in front of me and put that picture she asked me to bring in from when I was a kid. She said, "Now say those things to that little girl." I would never talk to my best friend this way. I needed to start being my own best friend.

I discovered four "power" words, and they are: I believe in you. The three power words are: I love you, and I like you. Words that always hurt are I told you so.

It wasn't easy, but slowly, my speech was coming back. That didn't stop me from trying to get my point across or my two cents in! I asked my husband for his feedback on how I talked. As he laughed, he said not much different than before! I was confused. He said, "Okay, let me give you an example."

Husband: Tells the story to the point in three minutes.
- Including key points only

Me: Telling the "exact" same story in 20 minutes.
- 25 insignificant details
- 11 back stories
- remembering I needed to add something to our grocery list.
- trying to get back on track by saying, "Where was I" about seven times.
- three off-topic stories
- four times saying, "To make a long story short."
- I'll finish later.

Well, that pretty much sums it up!

WAIT: **W**hy **A**m **I** **T**alking? I used to ask myself before I said something to others or myself.

Find something to be grateful for

We drove home from one of my appointments, and I looked at my windshield and there were splattered bugs stuck on it; I mean, it looked like a bug cemetery! Great, I thought as I went back into the house. When I looked outside, it was raining, I mean pouring. The downpour was only about 10 minutes before the sun started peeking out. I went back to my car, and the windshield was clean! I was never so grateful for the rain for washing off my bug guts, so I could see and didn't have to deal with them myself. Who would have thought such a little thing would be something I would be so grateful for? That's when I looked back on my life and realized even in the darkest of times, I had something to be grateful for.

I've been told that my journey may be the roadmap that could help someone else. My childhood made me mature far beyond my years. Surviving my car accident forced me to hit a bottom that allowed me to get the help I needed to deal with my husband's death. As I held him in my arms while he died, I experienced a life-changing moment of the most profound love you could ever imagine as he passed from this world to the next.

Through our marriage, I discovered what true love and commitment were, and I was able to remarry and have two more kids, knowing it was possible. The blessing of my illness showed me that through pain, you can learn to be resilient and explore other methods of healing, even if you think they are Woo-Woo!

I now have the opportunity to share what I know to help heal others. Holding on to the pain from your past is like a broken pencil; it's pointless. From learning how to talk during childhood and then re-learning after my illness, I gained the confidence to be an international speaker. I want to provide clarity to help you experience joy and pleasure, especially during those darkest moments.

> *Your ego says, "Once everything falls into place, I will find peace."*
> *Spirit says, "Find peace, and everything will fall into place." Unknown*

I questioned why I had to go through so much. That was until one day when I was feeling down on the anniversary of Rob's death, and my little girl grabbed my hand and said, **"I'm sorry your husband died, but if he didn't, you wouldn't be my mommy."** Need I say more?

Yes, I am grateful for each and every part of my life, even when they were painful, hurtful, nasty, delirious, and embarrassing, just to name a few ways. They didn't make me bitter; they made me better. We have one life to live, and don't you want to live the life you love?

By: Christa Rose
Ontario, Canada

Golden Nugget

"It's ok to give up HOPE standing for Heck Over Pleasing Everyone to Hold On Pain Ends."

About Author:

Name –Christa Rose

Contact – https://www.facebook.com/christa.rose.967

Christa is a distinguished Amazon #1 Bestselling Author, acclaimed for her book "Skip the Pain, Experience the Pleasure." Recognized for her dynamic and inspirational approach, she serves as a results-oriented Speaker, Certified Coach, Leadership Coach, Nutrition, and Health Advocate. She is certified in several modalities including Reiki, Intuitive Readings, and Akashic Records. She uses her profound experience to share her message, heal and change lives. She reveals her formula to show you how to go from chaos to clarity so you can experience happiness, peace, and joy even in the darkest times so you can live the life you love!

Chapter 9

Robyn Eyre-Long

A New Perspective

It's Valentine's Day, and I find myself grappling with self-doubt, questioning what sets me apart as extraordinary. Why should my light shine brighter than others? I acknowledge that many have achieved more significant feats than I have, prompting me to seek inspiration from Google on the essence of being extraordinary.

Resilience: Your ability to overcome challenges and bounce back from difficult situations.

Compassion: How you show empathy and kindness towards others, as well as your capacity for understanding and helping those in need.

Courage: The willingness to take risks, face fears, and stand up for what you believe in.

Generosity: Your capacity to give, share, and support others without expecting something in return.

Integrity: The consistency of your actions with your principles and values.

Self-Love: How well you take care of yourself mentally, emotionally, and physically.

Learning and Growth: Your openness to new experiences, willingness to learn, and commitment to personal development.

Positive Impact: The positive influence you have on the lives of those around you and in your community.

Achievements: Your personal and professional accomplishments, whether big or small.

Yes, I am all of these things, but so is every woman I meet. I see all these qualities in them, yet I struggle to see them in myself at times and even question why my experiences make me extraordinary.

When I asked my daughter what makes me extraordinary, she responded, "Mom, you've endured some of the toughest challenges, and you survived." While I acknowledge that many women have faced similar trials, I ponder: What truly distinguishes me as extraordinary?

As I reflect on this week, my mind recalls the individual and collective insights shared with me in various settings.

During a recent Zoom group session, a colleague of mine expressed her struggle with feelings of "not being good enough" and shared a dream featuring oversized work boots. This resonated with me, prompting the recollection of a story I often share during client sessions, particularly on the theme of self-forgiveness.

As I conveyed parts of this story to her, she remarked, "Robyn, your voice is that of a storyteller. You are a teacher with many wise words to share." I felt a deep sense of gratitude for this compliment, as it affirmed my inclination towards transitioning into teaching and mentoring, extending beyond one-on-one client interactions.

Tonight, a friend reached out and shared with me, "You are a light in the darkness for many! You call to the wounded and sing them into lullabies charged with healing and love! You listen to them weep, and you allow them the space to find themselves. You are a healer. A woman. A mother. You are a weaver of light, and you show all of us, through your authenticity and healing, how to weave our light back together and connect to our truth! You are a star map guiding those in the depths of their abyss. You have helped so many. You have touched so many. You are truly extraordinary."

With these words, I acknowledge how extraordinary I am in my own way. I don't need to compare myself to others. I am the best version of myself, striving to improve physically, mentally, emotionally, and spiritually every day, becoming who I am truly meant to be. I am on my own path, one that I have chosen for my highest good.

I have endured mental and verbal abuse, abandonment, single motherhood, self-doubt, loneliness, debt, betrayal, slander, mistrust, physical ailments, weight issues, loss of loved ones, departure from religion, loss of friendships, projection of others' feelings/thoughts, lost memories, soul fragmentation, working all-nighters to pay the bills, crying myself to sleep, and, at times, loathing my own existence.

What is extraordinary is that I don't linger in that low and negative energy as I once did. I acknowledge it, feel it, and with the assistance of the Divine, transmute that energy into loving guidance and wisdom. This process provides me with a fresh perspective and a renewed outlook on moving forward in my life. How did I acquire this skill? Let's take a brief journey into the past...

One day, as I was at home working in my front office, just like any other typical day, a sudden onset of sadness washed over me. Within a few minutes, it shifted to happiness and then a turn of physical pain in my heart. I thought I was losing my mind—perhaps I had been working too late, and my body had reached its limit. Why was I feeling everything all at once, and were these emotions even mine? I reached out to a friend, and she helped me become aware that my empathic gift was coming online, revealing that I was clairsentient—possessing the ability to feel others' emotions. This was a lot to navigate initially, as I needed to learn to discern what was mine, what belonged to others, and how to protect myself from absorbing others' emotions.

Reiki was the starting point for my journey toward enlightenment about the energies of the Universe and understanding the flow of energies from one source to another. Reiki is a holistic healing practice that originated in Japan. It involves the channeling of universal life energy through the practitioner's hands to promote balance, relaxation, and well-being in the recipient. The word "Reiki" itself combines "rei," meaning universal or spiritual, with "ki," which represents life force energy. Practitioners believe that this energy, when directed intentionally, can stimulate the body's natural healing abilities and encourage a state of physical, mental, and emotional harmony.

Reiki was my guide in connecting with the Divine, safeguarding my energy, and understanding others' energy. Channeling this pure energy for self-healing and the healing of others became a profound passion. Through continued sessions, I built trust in myself, even when conveying challenging messages. Recognizing that these Divine messages were catalysts for enduring healing, I understood the importance of trusting and sharing them to offer clients profound opportunities for transformation.

I remember a particular session with a new client who had been referred to me for symptoms of depression. Having lost her husband to suicide, she had recently remarried, blending families, and welcoming a new addition. As I connected with her, a strong message came through that she struggled with accepting the new baby. It was a delicate situation, but I trusted in Spirit and myself and gently said, "You are struggling with this new baby."

She broke down in tears, relieved that her hidden struggle was finally acknowledged. Throughout the healing session, it became apparent that this baby had a spiritual connection with her first husband. The profound messages and healing facilitated a transformation and a new perspective of her realization, lifting her from depressive symptoms. A newfound desire emerged to embrace and bond with this beautiful child, uniting their family into a harmonious and complete whole.

As my abilities and gifts expanded, so did my thirst for knowledge. I delved into crystal healing, Mayan Light Language, Quantum Body Processing, Contract work, and pursued various certifications while connecting with mentors and fellow healers. During an energy healing conference in Salt Lake City, I encountered a couple, both hypnotherapists.

The husband, concerned about his wife feeling overwhelmed, introduced her and asked for assistance. She explained her experiences with intense sensations during shadow work, feeling like worms crawling through her body. I helped her release old energies, transmuting them to Mother Earth, freeing her from unsettling feelings. Elated, she expressed a desire to continue working with me, proposing a session exchange.

Until then, hypnosis had been associated with the entertaining acts at the State Fair, where people did amusing things on stage. However, as much as I believed in Reiki, my encounter with a fellow healer, a hypnotherapist, prompted me to give it a try. To my amazement, in just 30 minutes, a belief I had been grappling with for some time was illuminated in a new way. This transformative experience captivated me, and I yearned to learn more. I enrolled as one of her students and, the following year pursued a Master Hypnosis Certification that emphasized the emotional healing aspect.

My exploration into hypnosis not only expanded my understanding of emotional healing but also shed light on the innate gift I possessed— the ability to perceive and comprehend multiple perspectives. The realization dawned during a couples counseling session in my married life, where the concept of perception began to unfold. This understanding was further solidified through our family's love for hockey. In the context of a game, when the on-ice official signaled a penalty, everyone involved—officials, players, coaches, scorekeepers, and spectators—held a distinct perspective on the incident. What struck me was the acknowledgment that each perspective was valid without one being inherently wrong. This ability to embrace diverse viewpoints without judgment became my gift and, at times, my challenge. Over the years, I've come to cherish this aspect of myself more and more.

The adage that the teacher learns more than the student genuinely holds, and the same dynamic unfolds between the healer and the receiver. With every healing session I facilitate, I am consistently astonished by the profound messages embedded in their healing journey—messages that often hold personal significance for me. This ongoing exchange expanded my perspectives, enabling me to discern the challenges clients faced in decision-making and foresee the potential outcomes of each choice. Armed with this insight, I empower my clients to grasp the implications of their decisions, both for themselves and their loved ones.

This approach not only enhanced my decision-making process but also deepened my understanding of the interconnectedness of choices and their impact on both personal and collective well-being. It became a transformative tool, allowing me to navigate life with a heightened sense of awareness and compassion.

Over the past year, I have been fascinated with the exploration of Human Design. As a Generator and Alchemist, I generate inspiring ideas and patiently seek confirmation from my outer world through sacral authority before acting. With a 3/5 profile, I embody the roles of an Explorer and Visionary Leader. My learning process involves understanding what doesn't work through life experiences, using that wisdom to generate energy, and guiding others toward their full potential. This system, combining elements of astrology, iChing, chakra systems, mysticism, and quantum physics, has added a valuable layer to my self-awareness and decision-making.

Understanding my Human Design has brought clarity to my life's purpose. I've realized that my journey is about experiencing all facets of life and gaining wisdom from both positive and challenging situations. Reflecting on this, I gave my son a gift at his high school graduation with the inscription, "Life is wisdom, good or bad; it is something to learn from." Unbeknownst to me, then, this encapsulates my life purpose: to experience, learn, and utilize that wisdom to empower clients, facilitating the transformation of old thought patterns and beliefs.

Recently, I encountered a situation where I faced verbal attacks in a group setting. My integrity was questioned, and the leader expressed distrust in me. The reactions of others in the group conveyed shock and disbelief. Post-meeting, some approached me to apologize, although I reassured them it wasn't necessary.

During this incident, I observed the group leader, as a scared individual desperately seeking acceptance, resorting to bullying to appear more relevant and overshadowing the embarrassment of not knowing all the procedures that he has touted for years that he knows intimately. This marked significant personal growth within me. A year ago, my response might have been defensive, but this time, I took a deep breath, stood in my truth, and allowed the situation to unfold without retaliation.

My aspiration for my clients, friends, and loved ones is for them to be so secure in who they are that no words can shake their foundation. Through regular meditation, healing practices, mentoring, and connecting with others, my own foundation has become increasingly firm. My perspectives and intuition grow more robust, and I recognize this as a gift—an extraordinary gift that I can share with myself and others. I aim to assist them with heartfelt words that invoke healing through new perspectives and a shift in core beliefs.

As this day draws to a close, with a puppy at my feet and the quietness of the house enveloping me, I reflect on my words and find assurance in the myriad ways I am extraordinary.

Resilience: I have overcome numerous challenges, rising each day to tackle the next one.

Compassion: I lend a loving ear to hear what troubles hearts, offering words of encouragement and healing to soothe the soul.

Courage: I face my fears, recognizing that fear is the absence of knowledge, and I am always eager to learn more.

Generosity: I freely give my time to myself and others, supporting them to the best of my ability.

Integrity: I am honest and authentic in all I say and do.

Self-love: I affirm my love for myself daily, recognizing that this love grows stronger with each passing day.

Learning and Growth: I welcome the opportunity to learn more about myself and the world I inhabit.

Positive Impact: Through kind words, attentive listening, and even a gentle touch, I am confident that I touch lives each day.

Achievements: In the 14 years I have been a single mom, I have achieved more than in the 40 years before. I believe that our accomplishments become as powerful and worthy as the strength we feel within ourselves.

I'm grateful for the opportunity to write and share my perspective on what I've learned and accomplished over the years. I hope that these words touch at least one person, letting them know they are supported, heard, seen, and felt. If I can be of any assistance, I'm just a call or email away.

I am committed to continuing my own path of healing and discovery so that I may mentor others with the wisdom I have gained. I aim to help others see a new perspective, a new light, and a new way of thinking, enabling them to achieve the profound happiness we all deserve in this life and those to come.

Blessings to all!!

Golden Nugget

"In every experience, there lies wisdom. Whether positive or negative, each moment offers lessons for learning and growth."

About Author:

Name – Robyn Eyre-Long

Contact – https://robyneyrelong.com/page/clearhealings

Robyn, the visionary behind Clear Healings, has over a decade of experience as a Transformation and Empowerment Mentor. Creator of the international virtual summit "I am Something Beautiful," she's an International Best-Selling Author and podcast guest. A Reiki Master, Intuitive Healer, and Master Hypnotherapist, Robyn guides others on transformative journeys. Her mentoring philosophy values forgiveness and perspective, believing everyone is inherently worthy. She helps individuals release past conditioning, embrace the present, and discover bliss, paving the way for authenticity, empowerment, and inner peace.

Chapter 10

Suzi Dent

Age-Defying Confidence:
The Power of Self-Belief at Any Stage

"I'm sure there are many women who are reading my story right now who can relate to being raised in a society where men felt entitled to touch women and girls without actually having their permission.

And that happened to me several times in my life, from the age of 12 to 23. So, as I was growing up, I tended to dress more like a tomboy. And I would wear baggy clothes and cover up my body. I wasn't comfortable wearing dresses and high-heeled shoes, I felt that I lost all my confidence when I wore dresses, and I felt exposed and unsafe. I never showed my cleavage or a bra strap or anything like that; I was raised in a very modest way. I didn't like to bring unwanted attention to myself from men, so from the age of 19, I covered myself up, and I moved through life feeling safer that way.

I also kept most of the unwanted touching a secret, as many of us do. I didn't tell my parents when I was 12 out of fear, as I thought I would get blamed. And we do that; we take on the responsibility as children for what adults do to us because the adults don't take responsibility for their actions.

When sexual assault and unwanted touching happen to us in our childhood, it changes the trajectory of our lives. When we keep things inside ourselves and don't use our voices to tell someone, they fester and grow, and they can hold us back from reaching our full potential. This kind of happened to me. The only way we actually start to heal is when we speak, then we can really start to deal with these things, learn how to heal from them, and actually give ourselves the gift of forgiveness.

From the age of 21, working as a freelance professional film and TV hair and makeup artist brought me boundless joy, as each job presented unique creative opportunities, ensuring I was never bored but always highly stimulated, constantly challenged to think on my feet and push the boundaries of my creativity. Working in studios and on location, I wore shorts and jeans and t-shirts and runners, so my tomboy dress sense fitted in perfectly. Forty years later, I am still employed and passionate about my craft.

In my fifties, as I navigated the tumultuous journey of menopause, I found myself grappling with waves of self-doubt and insecurities, questioning my worth and purpose. Coupling my doubts with the strain of an unhappy marriage with an angry husband, each day felt like a monotonous repetition of sameness in a life that seemed to have no hope. I couldn't see any light at the end of the proverbial tunnel; it was just darkness. I had this realization that I was ripping myself off, that I did not want to reach 70 having never experienced the glamour and femininity of feeling beautiful and wearing a beautiful gown, something that I had given to thousands of bridal clients over the decades.

It was really not a good existence. I was very unhappy. I was losing my natural, joyous self. And my really high vibrating energy was really rock bottom; I wasn't doing very well.

So, I started listening to motivational speakers when I went on my daily walks, and it was very inspiring. And I learned that we alone are responsible for how we feel and it is actually up to us to make changes in our lives. And if we really want to change, we have to make ourselves uncomfortable.

I put it out to the universe that I would like to be in front of the camera rather than behind it for a change. I used to sing in bands when I was younger and had lots of self-confidence, even though my self-esteem was low. Two weeks later, the universe answered my wish.

This was 2016, and I was nearly 55. I was approached by a woman who was the director of the Mrs Earth Australia beauty pageant. She had seen a photo of me online advertising my services as a makeup artist, and she contacted me to tell me that they thought I would be a really good fit as a pageant contestant. I literally fell off the bed laughing because I hadn't worn a dress for 30 years, and I didn't actually own a pair of high-heeled shoes, never mind being able to walk in them.

As an award-winning makeup artist, I had headed up the team for the Miss Universe pageant. I loved watching the girls and all the glamour, but never once had I ever dreamed of being a contestant. However, I was intrigued and flattered to be asked, so I checked out the pageant and the charity they supported, and I realized that my prayers had really just been answered. I was having my own sliding doors moment!

I could stay where I was in life, feeling unhappy and unfulfilled while ignoring this incredible gift that was being given to me, or I could say yes to the most out-of-left-field thing that I had ever been asked and trust that the universe had my back.

And I realized that God had sent me this gift. And that I had to trust and say yes to it. I didn't ask my husband. I just said yes. And in saying yes, I changed the trajectory of my life.

Over the previous 30 years, I had developed this kind of psychological fear of wearing dresses; I was very uncomfortable wearing anything fitted because it really did feel like I lost my power and all my confidence would drain out of me. And I really did feel exposed. And I've spoken to women over the years who have felt similarly, and they've dressed down and covered themselves up, too. It's a trauma response.

I am a bit of a go-getter. Being self-employed since I was 19 gives me the confidence and fearlessness to attempt new endeavors. When I do something, I always give it my all.

I started embracing the world of pageantry and researching all about it. And each day, I would visualize myself on a stage with my name being called out as the winner. I would fill myself up with the gratitude and excitement of becoming Mrs. Earth Australia, and I believed it 100 percent. Even though I was the oldest competitor, I didn't let that stop me in any way. I knew that this was my journey, so I just went for it.

I got myself sponsored by an international company. I was their ambassador around the world. And they gave me a PR agent. I spoke at business breakfasts and women's groups about the charity I was supporting – Soles4Souls to create awareness, raise funds, and collect new and used shoes to distribute to those who had none.

My husband loved what I was doing; it really invigorated our relationship, and he enjoyed shopping for dresses online that I would feel comfortable in to speak on stages. I had a sash and a tiara that became my superpower, so whenever I wore them, I became Mrs. Earth. People would always approach me with curiosity and ask me questions, so any nervousness or trepidation I had about speaking about my journey or the charity went away.

I had sponsors come to me who also believed in my success, which was awesome: a dress designer, a personal trainer, a photographer, and a cosmetics company. Life had provided everybody I needed to ensure my success.

The final arrived, and there were several sections that I had to get top marks in to win the overall title: Interview, charity; I had to make an outfit out of recycled material, casual wear and of course, evening gown.

I had a gown made, so it fit me perfectly. It was my design, and for my very first gown, it was super important that I felt confident and beautiful, which I sure did!

I like to say that I cured my fear of dresses, one frock at a time!

I am humbled and proud to say that I was announced the winner and was crowned the first Mrs. Earth Australia 2017, competing against 18 other women of all ages from around the country at the age of 55.

That night, I started giving press interviews, and the world sat up and loved my story of mid-life transformation, the 55-year-old tomboy to beauty queen. I found myself on morning talk shows, in magazines, and in newspapers around the world. It was amazing; I was also inspiring older women to take a leap of faith, trust in themselves, and do different things. As a natural beauty, botox and filler-free, my pro-aging stance and mantra of "Age is Just a Number" was being heard and celebrated.

The following three months found me learning to walk in 6-inch stilettos, the pageant heels we are all required to wear, and for two weeks, I would just stand in them at the end of my bed on the carpet to get my balance and get used to how big they were. I practiced every day. I perfected my balance, learned how to glide from the hip, and graduated to tiles and wooden floors.

I had an interview coach, one of the best in the world of pageantry, and learned how to craft my speech and answers to fit what was required in pageantry. I was doing interviews, speaking on stages, and representing and promoting the charity and my sponsors. It filled my life, my heart, and my soul as I raised my self-esteem to high levels of confidence and found my true, authentic self along the way.

Three months later, I found myself in Las Vegas, representing Australia in the 4th biggest international pageant system. I competed against 36 women from around the world who ranged from the ages of 21, with me being the second oldest.

I was standing there on the stage in the middle of my own very surreal fairytale. Half the women that were there with me, I could have given birth to.

And as an older woman and a newly minted dress wearer, It was an amazing life-changing experience. I never let my age or my inner tomboy cause any doubt that I belonged there or hold me back in any way; I just embraced this amazing experience with joy and gratitude.

I took this numbing cream with me, the sort you use if you get tattoos, and I put it all over my feet so I couldn't even feel my feet when I walked out on that stage. I didn't want to fall over and face-plant the stage in front of the world and let Australia down. And I didn't.

I won third place and was crowned Mrs. Earth Health, which blew me away.

I was inundated with press around the world; I had a blast!

Two hours after I arrived home in Australia, I welcomed a camera crew and reporter who interviewed me at my house for our biggest morning show. I then got to talk about ageism in society and living your best life and not letting age or society's constructs of your age be a personal barrier that actually holds you back from being the person that you are meant to be.

Because Age is Just a Number! You can be fit, young, strong, and vital as you age by paying attention to the following disciplines. Live a life full of gratitude, exercise mindfulness, and be careful of the way you communicate to yourself about yourself. Words are powerful. Look after your body with regular exercise and a healthy diet; you only get one body, so take care of it.

Believing in yourself and diving into what you truly desire is key. Because unless you confront your fears head-on, you'll never unlock your full potential. Failure? It's just part of the journey. If you don't take a shot, you'll never know what you could achieve. And even if things don't work out, you'll gain invaluable lessons along the way.

The doors of motivational speaking opened to me all around the world. I became a sexual assault victims advocate in 2019. The world was ready to hear my story, and I was ready to tell it because becoming Mrs. Earth Australia had given me the experience that I needed to speak on stages and inspire others. I had the best coaches in the world, who taught me how to tell my story in the right way for media interviews. I had the confidence to dress the way that society expects us to dress.

I used my voice, and I have been accepted beautifully around the world. I've had some amazing interviews and met awesome people who have changed my life along the way. I feel incredibly blessed to have the journey that I've had and for transforming into the diamond that I always was inside.

In 2023, the UK press dubbed me the "Voice For Millions" for my discussions on Operation Yewtree's societal impact. As a witness in a groundbreaking sexual assault court case, I contributed to history. It marked the first time victim-survivors of historical crimes in the entertainment industry were truly heard, leading to the criminal convictions of influential figures who misused their power. This pivotal moment in 2014 sparked the #MeToo movement.

Speaking up is how we drive societal change. When we hear others share their voices, it fosters solidarity and empowers us. Just reaching out to one person can kickstart your healing journey—it's that crucial. Personally, I've spoken to audiences worldwide, reaching over 30 million people, and had the privilege of being featured in two international documentaries.

As I close this chapter of my journey, I stand as living proof that age is just a number. Gratitude, mindfulness, and positive self-talk have been my trusted companions, guiding me through life's highs and lows. From my days as Mrs. Earth Australia to becoming a fierce advocate for survivors of sexual assault, my path has been one of transformation and empowerment.

Sharing my story on the global stages has shown me the immense power of speaking up. Being hailed as the "Voice For Millions" by the UK press reaffirmed the importance of amplifying voices and sparking change. I've learned that true strength lies not only in my own voice but in uplifting others to share theirs.

At 62, I'm more determined than ever to continue lighting the way forward. Let's journey together towards a world where every voice matters, every survivor is supported, and every individual is empowered to shine bright.

Golden Nugget

"Age is Just a Number"

About Author:

Name – Suzi Dent

Contact – https://suzident.com/

I'm Suzi Dent, an internationally acclaimed, award-winning speaker and author, dedicated to helping you illuminate your story and elevate your voice. With years of expertise, I empower people to shine in media interviews, conferences, personal storytelling and life. Beyond mentoring, I'm also a multi award winning film and television hair and makeup artist and special effects artist with 40 years of experience in the entertainment industry. As the inaugural Mrs. Earth Australia, at age 55, I led by example, by embodying the belief that age is just a number, inspiring others to step out of their comfort zone and embrace their full potential.

Chapter 11

Donna Sparaco Meador

How to MasterDate™ - Thriving After
Loss or Divorce

In a twist I never anticipated, I found myself married to two
men – simultaneously.

I know...It's not what you think.

After a short-lived marriage, I eventually met and married the man of my dreams. And... after his passing, I found myself venturing back into the dating scene again at 58.

As a young teenager, I dreamed of a fulfilling relationship with a man, capturing my sentiments in a poem featured in my first book, *"DATING: It's Not Personal."* Today, that book is also a love story, offering the nuts and bolts of how I met and married my late husband, Pietro.

"Until death due you part is a fallacy." I remember thinking, *"How can I fall in love when I'm already in love?"* It never dawned on me that I could meet a second Mr. Wonderful and walk down the aisle again.

Before I met Pietro over twenty years ago, I found myself single and dating in my early 40s. At that time, I had little understanding of my own value, accepting far too little, for far too long, clinging to relationships with men I didn't even like. In the three years that followed, I learned a great deal about myself, discovering not only what I wanted but, more importantly, what I didn't want. This process brought forth confidence, self-respect, and the ability to established boundaries.

One day in 2007, this debonair man walked into my life. Pietro was a simple man, a romantic, and the man of my dreams. He was born in Italy, and even after 50 years here in the States, he still had that beautiful Italian accent. You never saw a picture of him without a smile, a cigar in, or a glass of red. He didn't argue to make a point. He felt people would know who he was by his actions. And he was right. Who he was spoke volumes, especially to me.

Pietro helped me understand the importance of putting each other first. And always said, "At the end of the day, Bella Mia, it's-a-you, and it's-a-me." And at the end of the day, it always was.

One clear, warm morning toward the end of summer, I received an unexpected phone call. Pietro's voice, shaky and strained, told me he had coughed up blood. That was the day our lives changed forever. Three short months later, while he was undergoing treatment, I got another call: Pietro had suffered a heart attack and a stroke instantaneously. The moment he collapsed; my world collapsed.

It's difficult to explain how I felt when Pietro died. I didn't faint as much as I crumbled. If you've ever lost someone close to you, you might know what I'm talking about. *Everything changes, and yet nothing changes.* You can't squeeze them or hold them or kiss them ... but well, you can rearrange the furniture without anyone saying anything.

They say, "Love never dies." If this is true, then what do you do when the need for love reappears? I was about to find out.

Eight months after his passing, upon an introduction to a man I'd never met (and never saw again), as we stood there shaking hands, tingles ran through my entire body – and right there in the middle of a business meeting, *I GOT TURNED ON.*

HOLY CRAP!

I was like a deer in headlights! My heart started to pound! My fingers got sweaty!

— I was like a blooming 16-year-old and thought for sure everyone in the room was staring at me. On my drive home, I was jumping out of my skin with excitement - until I got home and remembered.

A handful of months after that incident, I decided to begin dating again, and it was for one thing and one thing only. I was planning to keep my HEART OUT of it and my BODY IN it *(if you know what I mean)*.

"Norms," as you are referred to, if you haven't lost a spouse, tend to think there's an acceptable time frame for such things, an acceptable way to be. Not true. Time has no meaning at a time like this.

Every day that passed meant I was one day further away from my late husband.

Trying to understand grief can help you process it as you muddle through or as you watch someone you care about go through it. For me, I decided to share my grieving in real-time on social media. It was extremely therapeutic for me, and I hoped it would help others as well. Amid grieving, with no walls or curtains to hide behind, people were tuning in as I went live on social media. The show eventually became known as *Daily Dose A Donna*.

I was raw, real, and deliberate about looking for happiness where it was and not where it wasn't. Every day, I felt a little better as I began to recognize the gifts bestowed upon me, like a hug from Pietro's granddaughter, for example, or a phone call from someone who knew him years ago with their heartfelt memories.

People watching seemed to be in awe as I was putting one foot in front of the other. I was conscientiously setting my inner dial to joy smack in the face of the hardest thing I've ever had to do in my life. Why? Because feeling worse was not an option.

Through all of it, these phases of grief that everyone talks about kept running through my mind. They seemed incomplete. There's denial, anger, bargaining, depression, and acceptance. As you might know, they don't necessarily pop in and out in order, but somehow, it makes it easier if you recognize them. Even so, there was still something missing for me. The ONE and ONLY THING I was curious about, was missing: That insane, overwhelming urge I felt at that business meeting.

I mean, SEX is EVERYWHERE, and suddenly, *poof!* It's nowhere to be found at a time like this, when you want to be held, not by your friends. Not a pat on the back. But held. Desired! This thought wouldn't go away. There are all kinds of psychosomatic mumbo jumbo about how long these phases may or may not take, but nothing about looking for, desiring, or even *wanting*, nuki-nuki? *How is that possible? How is it that sex and intimacy got omitted OR, more accurately, were never included in the phases of grieving? One of the strongest emotions we universally have, and there's no talk about it.*

How is it that there's no discussion about how it can mess with you now that your lover has crossed over to the other side? *Not a peep on how to process it, OR like in my case,* how long the LACK of desire might continue...

So why am I talking about this? Well, number 1) If you're grieving the loss of a partner, I think it's safe to assume you're an adult. Sex used to be taboo when I was a kid, but today, we are well into the new millennium. Then, 2) Don't you think people would be best served if it was an obvious conversation, hanging out in the open and talked about like a crisp bedsheet hanging on the clothesline on a beautiful, windy Spring Day?

It's my feeling that love and the desire for intimacy, whether you want it or not, should be a bullet point along with the other phases. Then we will all know we're not alone. I had no clue that anyone would even want sex after loss, let alone desire it immediately. I thought the numbness I was experiencing was what everybody felt. Additionally, I had zero idea as to how long it would last.

So, there I was, talking about this taboo topic (indiscreetly, of course. After all, this was social media), and women were reaching out to me looking for advice. Some told me they would never meet another like their beloved, so should they even try? It seemed they needed permission, as if loving another would somehow dismiss the love they had before. My friends, loving another doesn't replace anyone.

The ability to love two men at the same time is, admittedly, hard to understand. Certainly, for the "wid" going through this, and often for any offspring, whatever their age. Parents, siblings, and friends can all be confused when you fall in love - again. They wonder how you can fall in love so quickly or – at all?

My friends, whether you're single again due to divorce or loss or have never been married and you are ready to focus on your personal life, I've got you. I've been there. I've been divorced, and I've been widowed.

If you're a widow who doesn't know where to start, a divorcee ready to dip your toe back in the water, or just someone getting back out there and has no idea what to do, I want you to know I've been in your shoes and am eager to assist you on your journey.

You won't resonate with my message if you're not seeking a heartfelt connection or if you harbor negative feelings towards men. I adore men. It's just brilliant to allow those that resonate with you to rise to the surface. So, if you're turned off or still angry, I hope you'll seek me out when you're ready.

"How did you manage to find love twice in a row?" is the question I am frequently asked, and I promise to delve into that shortly. But before we get into the nitty-gritty, it's crucial to remember the age-old adage: happiness stems from within. We've all heard it countless times, but it took me experiencing life's highs and lows to comprehend its significance genuinely. It was through this journey that I embarked on a path of self-discovery and inner growth—a journey that often serves as the genesis of our true endeavors.

If you're pondering the essence of a genuine connection, then kudos to you—it's an excellent inquiry. Whether it's casual encounters, committed relationships, or anything in between, the choice is entirely yours. My role here is to guide you through the sometimes-murky waters of modern dating. Many of us find ourselves at a crossroads, wondering, "What now, what's next," and feeling a bit overwhelmed or uncertain. Let me assure you that if you're experiencing trepidation or insecurity, you're not alone. Because let's face it—DATING is not for wussies.

Today, I'm affectionately known as the Smart Dating Diva Queen, specializing in relationship alignment. My forte lies in aiding single, soul-searching women in discerning whether to pursue or bid adieu within the initial four dates. While some individuals may never discover true love, I, using my own methodology, found it not once but twice.

Enter the S.M.A.R.T. process—an acronym representing the pillars of positioning yourself for pursuit, navigating with self-awareness, and recognizing your inherent worth. Trust that if a man is genuinely interested in dating you, he will make an effort to go above and beyond for the one who captures his attention.

If you're ready to embrace new possibilities and navigate the realm of dating with an intelligent and pain-free approach, you're in the right place.

I've had the privilege of enjoying a fulfilling life with my late husband, Pietro. And yes, I took the plunge down the aisle once again at the age of 60, now reveling in the joys of married life with my husband, Jeffrey. Together, we share playful moments and daily laughter. I often joke that we sing together, although he's the one with the melodic voice—I'm more of the background dancer in this dynamic duo. We've even joined forces to create a TV show.

Now, let's rewind to the early days of my dating journey—a period rife with trials and tribulations, which I bravely navigated so that you don't have to. You can delve into those escapades in my first book, "DATING: It's Not Personal." A pivotal component of dating is acknowledging the diversity in our strengths and weaknesses. It serves as a poignant reminder that dating is not a personal affront. Instead, it's an opportunity for growth and enjoyment.

Women often express their reluctance to relinquish their independence or submit to external influence. However, true partnership transcends mere companionship; it's founded on friendship. As someone who values independence and drive, I can attest to the profound strength I derive from Jeff's unwavering support. Together, we embody the essence of teamwork—recognizing that our combined efforts yield infinitely more significant results than those achieved individually.

My journey through the dating landscape wasn't without its challenges. However, through years of observation, countless conversations, and actual dating experiences, I developed a systematic approach. This approach empowered me to make informed decisions regarding the continuation or conclusion of a connection before the fourth date—a milestone I deemed worthy of conferring upon myself the title of "Doctorate in Dating™."

Today, I've documented this system, eager to empower other single women re-entering the dating scene because I've been in their shoes—twice.

Furthermore, feel free to explore our free app, "Meador & Meador," available on your App or Play Store. There, you'll not only discover a delightful blend of ever-growing relational tips and entertaining banter between Jeff and me, but then can be notified when new content is downloaded.

So, how did I manage to find love twice in a row? It all boils down to consciously directing my thoughts and energy toward the positive aspects of the relationship I desired. By fostering a mindset that attracted individuals aligned with my values and preferences, I manifested the love I sought. In essence, I focused on what I desired for myself rather than dwelling on what I didn't. This proactive approach not only shaped my perspective on love but also played a pivotal role in attracting fulfilling and compatible connections.

Yes, seeking love where it truly resides—within oneself—is the key to mastering the art of dating.

Golden Nugget

"Look for love where it is, and not where it's not."

About Author:

Name – Donna Sparaco Meador

Contact – https://meadorandmeador.com/

Donna Sparaco Meador is known as the Smart Dating Diva QUEEN specializing in Relationship Alignment.

She is a Speaker / Author / Women's Dating Coach & Founder of S.M.A.R.T. Dating. Donna found true love again, after the passing of her late husband. Her forte lies in aiding single, soul-searching women to know within the initial four dates whether to continue or bid them adieu.

Donna won the "Greatest Soulful Speaker" award at the 2023 Soulful Speaker Summit, the Winner of the Forbes Riley 2020 "Power Couple of Excellence" Award with her husband Jeff and is Co-creator & Co-Host of the television show "THE MEADOR AFFECT" due out soon!

Chapter 12

Dar Geiger

Being God's Joyologist

I have a confession to make... I'm not always happy!
But...

I got the joy, joy, down in my heart... Do you have joy in your heart? Or is it missing in your life?

What is joy, and where does it come from? Happiness is dependent on our circumstances. Joy is not. It comes from a relationship with God and is always with us regardless of our circumstances.

Why choose joy? Because it will keep your mind, body, and relationships healthy, and so much more!

I'm going to share a significant tool that will help you experience joy even when going through trials. It's called gratitude. It's based on my story of recovery from addictions, the loss of my soulmate, breast cancer, and how I became a messenger for you.

Have you ever experienced a time in your life where you went from being extremely happy to absolute despair in a matter of minutes? My husband, Chuck, and I were soulmates. We met in 7th grade!

We were celebrating our 45th wedding anniversary in October of 2006 and were discussing the awesome three weeks we had in July touring Norway, where my ancestors are from. My husband—who is such a joker—suddenly slumped over on the table... I started laughing and said, "Honey, what are you doing?" But he did not move.

I looked, and the joy immediately left me. I was shocked! He wasn't breathing! I asked God for help and immediately dialed 911. They told me to lay him on the floor and give him CPR, and for ten minutes, I pumped his heart and kept on praying: "Dear God, please save my husband." The ambulance came and took us to the hospital... he had a 100% blockage in a main artery. My family and friends prayed for God to save Chuck's life. A miracle happened, and he was spared. For eight weeks of rehab, we were hopeful about his progress and thought he was going to survive... but his heart gave out, and he was gone!

My world crashed! I never felt like I wanted to end my life, but I didn't want to live anymore. With a broken heart, I chose to pray and trust: "Dear God, please be with me. I don't want to be a widow, but I'm thankful for the many years we had."

While reading the Bible, my daughter was convicted to give away her belongings, and she and her 4-year-old son moved in with me. That was a blessing. I felt hope. Having my little grandson and daughter living with me helped me feel loved and brought a spark of—you guessed it—joy and purpose! There is life after loss!!

After a while, my daughter and I decided we were going to invite friends to do a Bible study... but you know what happened? We came together, and we ended up belly-laughing. It was exactly what we all needed. We knew we needed to laugh, so we decided to play and praise God. The Bible says in...

Nehemiah 8:10 says that the "joy of the Lord is our strength."

We called ourselves the "Ladies of Laughter" - LOL—and we would have a different theme each month. One month, the theme was to dress as tacky as possible, and it was a hoot! We came together to laugh—laughter heals our minds and body. Ask for support—you just might get it!

Later, I decided to attend a program called "Grief Share," which helped me work through the pain of the loss of my husband. It taught me that when I least expected it, I would be ambushed by memories and would cry uncontrollably. I never knew when it was going to hit. I learned to be gentle with myself, and that it hurt so bad because I loved so hard. It helped me recover... over time, and I began to heal and had a purpose in life to live for God, family, and friends.

About four years later, in 2010, I had another shock...

I was told that I had breast cancer and said, "Really, God? After losing my husband? I can't do this... I was so scared." I prayed, and God gave me a scripture that I held close to my heart:

Psalm 34:4: "I cried out to the Lord; He heard my cry and delivered me from all my fear."

I know there are people out there who have gone through cancer or have been diagnosed, and some of you may never have had it, and I hope you never will, but it's terrifying. I decided that I was going to trust God's love and word and felt thankful for that scripture. Then I went through surgery. Afterward, I had to lie still and not move for 20 minutes on the radiation table for treatment. Now, I am a Type A personality and relatively energetic, and I thought, "Lord, how am I going to lie on that table for 20 minutes and not move? I need your help."

Then, one day in one of those sessions, I had an encounter that I will never forget:

I was on the table and decided to turn my head away and imagine talking to God—I had to look away because the radiation was going right over my heart. I started talking and said: "Lord, help me. My life is yours..." and I heard Him say: "Darlene, you're my 'joy-giver'... I want you to share my love and joy with others by telling your story... it will help them find joy."

I was stunned... I thanked Him and took it to heart. When you recognize your purpose, focus on it! I learned through this journey that there are powerful tools available for us to navigate through trials and experience hope and joy. Be willing to ask for help... Then take a risk and give your problem over and say: "God, I give my problem to you. I'm going to trust you." Then let it go.

Once you do this, you're going to feel free from worry, which helps you be more open to noticing things to be thankful for. For example, there's clinical proof that laughter is so good for you. If you can't laugh, ask, and make a place for it to happen!

When I was addicted to shopping, it caused problems, but it also taught me to laugh at myself. Have you ever been on a shopping quest where you're finding bargains everywhere, so you put everything else aside, including your body's call to function? Well, I was on an emotional high because of all the bargains... I really needed the bathroom, but I didn't want to stop.

You guessed it... I waited too long, and in a panic, looked for the restroom and ran into the room barely in time... a minute later, I heard the weirdest sound on the floor... clink... I looked under my stall and saw a man's belt buckle... on top of a man's pants... on top of a man's shoes... yikes... I'm in the men's bathroom... get me out of here. I was mortified. After a few minutes of recovery... you know what? I felt grateful that I made it to the bathroom in time. I realized the more gratitude I found, the more I experienced joy. So, I laughed and told myself not to take myself too seriously and went back to shopping!

One of the most important ways to navigate through trials and have genuine joy is to learn about what gratitude can do for you. It means you're willing to watch for something that warms your heart or makes you smile. For example, a beautiful sunrise or sunset or putting your feet on the floor in the morning... which means you're alive. How about the fragrance of that first cup of coffee? I'm so thankful for music and dancing. I dance to my favorite music at home most days... it makes me happy! There's clinical proof of what gratitude will do for us mentally and physically. It helps to keep you from going into a downward spiral of darkness. I want you to see gratitude as a treasure chest and that you are about to discover something that everyone wants and needs... and that is genuine joy.

I challenge you to learn from my experiences and seek it with all your heart. I would love to hear what you find.

Golden Nugget

> "If what you say, doesn't come from your heart,
> it will not reach the listeners!"

About Author:

Name – Dar Geiger
Contact – https://www.facebook.com/dargeiger1

I am an Author, Speaker & Joyologist. I'm passionate about working with people who are searching for substance and joy while going through life's trials. I equip them with tools and principles that inspire and empower them when trials occur. This is based on my story of recovery from addictions, the loss of 2 soulmates, breast cancer & how I became a Joyologist for others.

Chapter 13

Soné Swanepoel
Voiceless No More

Being created as a Helper, I was called on this journey of life to find my voice and my worth. I was called to understand the pain and challenges that come from being voiceless and not realizing your worth. I was born into a loving family with amazing parents who always did their best for me. I was and still am very close to my family. Yet, I grew up voiceless, not because anyone was evil or ill-meaning, but because it is part of my purpose. To understand the value of the voice, to empower others and lead the way, to show the light, and for others to also find their voice and value themselves. I want to start by highlighting that my story is my perception of how my life unfolded. I in no way pass blame to anyone or regret anything that happened on my life journey to date.

For many years, I believed that I was not good enough. I went to a doctor in 2022 who helped me pinpoint where my belief of not being "good enough" came from. This belief was created unconsciously when I was four years old - when my mother fell pregnant with my sister. I believed I was not good enough; it was never said or indicated in the least, but that was the belief system that was unconsciously formed in my little head. It was an unfounded belief, but it was still created. Over the years, experiences and defining moments reinforced the idea that I was not good enough.

Not feeling worthy made me very sensitive. Someone could look at me funny or sideways, and I would take it personally and cry. It did not help that I was a shy little girl who would not speak to you if you did not speak to me first. This lasted well into my adult years, mainly when I spoke to men or people in authority. I did not put much value into my own opinions or knowledge of myself and my needs – I outsourced them.

I was raised in an era where it was said: "Children are seen and not heard," and I fully bought into that. Don't get me wrong; I had a certain type of confidence growing up, but not the type that enabled me to stand up or speak up for myself. I did speak and have an opinion, except when it would lead me to get into "trouble," to conflict, or when it was outside of my safe space. Being voiceless, I was unable to stand up for myself and used tears or silent treatment to protect myself.

I was bullied in school, and I did not realize the impact of this until many years later. It contributed to my becoming a people-pleaser, who was what friends wanted me to be, just so that I would not be rejected. Later friendships would see me having no boundaries and overextending myself, all in an effort for outside validation and acceptance.

My mother has placed me on various diets since I was 12 years old. I was a bit chubby, but nothing excessive. It knocked my self-confidence and probably further enforced the idea that I was not good enough the way that I was. I needed to be thin to be loved and accepted.

My mother did it with the best of intentions; my dad's side of the family had some big ladies, and my mother did not want me to end up like that. However, knowing that did not help my subconscious mind; my subconscious mind coupled my worth and value to my weight. This was just another area of my life where I did not have a voice. I was not able to say 'no.' That is not what I wanted. I wanted to keep my mother happy. I do not blame my mother or hold it against her. It was part of my journey, and she did the best she could with her knowledge. I love you, Mom.

When I got married, I went from an Obedient child to an obedient wife—I was a very obedient child, and when I got married, I became an obedient wife without a voice. Not because my husband did not "allow" me to speak but because I did not have the confidence or skill to express myself properly. I was also petrified of conflict and rejection, so the easiest thing was to keep quiet and ignore my needs.

I never really allowed people to get to know the real me. Experience taught me that it would leave me vulnerable and open to hurt. I was also afraid that the real me was not good enough. Past experiences have shown me that I had to lose weight to be better, do more, or be a better friend. Me, just as true me, I was not good enough.

So, I closed off and did not trust many people. I would agree with what others wanted or liked. Yes, I did have an opinion, and I raised it when I was in my comfort zone and felt safe, but if a different opinion meant conflict, no way, it was not worth getting hurt or rejected. I was, in any case, not able to order my thoughts properly when engaged in conflict or bring them over without crying.

I learned the power of silent treatment. It is a wonderful manipulation tool, but it made me sad and lonely. I had to go silent to get the attention I wanted or needed, and I did not have the skill to express myself properly to get my needs met.

I learned to do everything for myself and not depend on people. People let you down, and they hurt you. Use you for their needs (which I allowed because I did not have any boundaries) and then go on with their lives. I am not good at asking for help. I can see what others need, and I thought all people were like that. But I have learned that is not so. So again, because they could not gauge my needs and, therefore, fulfill them, I felt unworthy-not realizing that my inability to express myself correctly was part of the problem.

I believed I was like the ugly duckling. I looked in the mirror, and I saw a little girl with pigtails and freckles who was not as thin as the other girls. I remembered the story of the ugly duckling, and I hoped and believed that one day I would be like that little ugly duckling that was going to turn into the most beautiful swan. (Funny side note ... My married surname is Swanepoel ... can you see the 'swan' in the first part of my surname? It seems like the law of attraction has a very funny sense of humor ☺).

These are perhaps not significant things, but collectively, they added up and had a massive impact on my self-image, self-worth, and voice.

So where did this lead to?

I was born with a positive outlook on life and a smile on my face. It is part of my personality. As I grew up, God gently guided me to people, situations, books, lessons, and a desire to be more, not to be stuck in the box that my own belief systems placed me in. I wanted to be more and better than I was. I believe that we have many little things along the way that nudge us and guide us to start changing. It is not a once-off happening because we are never done changing, growing, and transforming.

Because I was so shy and sensitive and because I knew how debilitating and lonely that was, I never wanted my children to be shy. When I was about 35 years old, I looked at my amazing little girls and saw that they were becoming precisely what I did not want them to be. By that time, I had heard a bit about the power of the mind and the law of attraction; I realized that I had to change my views and belief systems, that I had to get that negative: "I don't want them to be" out of my head. I immediately let go of those thoughts and started working on how I wanted them to be.

I realized that I had to step up. I read part of the book: "Standing Up for Your Child Without Stepping on Toes" by Vicki Caruana. My AHA moment: "I am my children's only campaigner. If I do not stand up for them, fight for them, speak up for them – who will? It is up to me." That was a game-changer. My family is my second most important value in life; I needed to step up. I needed to be better. I needed to show them that I had their backs, no matter what, even if it meant stepping outside of my comfort zone. It was not easy; it never is.

What changed:

- I got my boundaries in place. 'Soné could not say "no," and she was a people pleaser.' I realized that I was allowing others to use me. Putting myself in positions where I am needed and would be appreciated – be validated. I did things at a cost to myself and my family. I got tired of being there for everyone, and it felt like everything was one-sided. I still remember my brother-in-law telling me one day: "Soné, you have to be fair. Not just to others but also to yourself." That hit home hard, and I started implementing it in my life. It started small, but it was very empowering.

- I worked on communicating more effectively. I wanted a better relationship with my husband, more intimate, where I could voice my needs and desires without fear of rejection. Every little thing that happened that I read and that I learned that made sense to me was valuable and shaped me; I worked on my ability to communicate and to be heard. I am blessed to have a husband who was, and still is, willing to listen and to change as well. It was a long journey but oh so worth it.

- I hated that I could not express myself and own my voice. I wanted to be able to communicate with others when there were conflicts without fear of being in trouble or being hurt or rejected. My throat just used to close up, and I could say nothing. I hated it. It was so devastating. I was tired of it. Somewhere along the line of my journey, I became better at expression. Everything that happened pushed me towards that.

- I had this inner guidance that led me to things to do. I know God directed my path the whole way. He brought the people, situations, courses, and everything I needed when I needed to become the person I wanted to be. I used to say that I wanted to be the best version of myself, but I changed it to the highest version of me. It became clear to me that when I am the best version of myself, I am who I think I can be. When I am the highest version of myself, I am who God created me to be.

- I changed my mindset toward shyness. I also had to step out of my comfort zone and be an example for my children. I found a theme song to build my confidence and make me feel better about my body and who I was. I learned to love and appreciate my body as it was—unconditionally and without any more conditions.

- I read self-help books and books on mindset and self-improvement.

- I started to become clear about the friends I wanted, the relationships I wanted, and my purpose in life. I let go of my "lack mindset" and focused on what I did have.

- I adopted the belief that I can grow old healthy and beautifully at every age. A mindset was changed, and my brain and body were bought into it. I started to lose my fat because I dealt with my emotional issues.

- I learned to love myself unconditionally. I accepted myself, the good, the bad, and the ugly.

- I learned to rely on myself to feel loved and happy and not to put that responsibility on others. I took ownership of my life and happiness; I no longer outsourced it.

- I value my thoughts and insights now. I worked hard to get them; I had difficult life lessons that I had to learn to earn my insights. I am worthy of trusting myself, especially when it comes to my needs, values, and worth.

- I learned the value of Coaching, both giving it and receiving it.

- What worked very well for me was writing a book. There is something about putting your thoughts to paper. It is liberating and releases feelings and emotions that you have buried and denied for so long. I realized what my triggers were, and I appreciated the lessons that I learned along the way. It ordered my thoughts and was one of my most significant healing tools. The name of my book is 1Life – Voiceless No More, and it is available on Amazon.

My superpowers and how I make the world a better place.

- I am a Helper; it is who I am and who I have always been. I have healed, and I want that for all women. I want them to have a voice and to love themselves unconditionally. To accept themselves. To find their worth in themselves and not look for it from others. To be truly happy with who and what they are. Not apologizing for who they are or their voice. To not feel guilty for putting themselves and their needs first. To have a safe space to let go and transform. To transform like a butterfly and be reborn like a phoenix. To acknowledge and appreciate the fire that they have been through and see them through my eyes – magnificent beings of strength, beauty, heart, and love.

- I have the ability to see the potential in other people. Through my coaching and speaking to other people in general, I help them see who they are meant to be and who they can be. I hold the space for them to become that person.

- I am positive, and I believe that everything that happens to me is a blessing. I choose to see every incident or experience as a stepping stone and not a stumbling block. Nothing keeps me down. It is all opportunities.

- I connect with people and listen without judgment.

- I make the world a better place by showing up as me, being a mirror for people, and being there for them when they need me while keeping my boundaries, talking the walk, and walking the talk.

Golden Nugget

"1 Life to live and be happy – Live it!"

About Author:

Name – Soné Swanepoel
Contact – www.soneswanepoel.com

I'm a Self-Awareness & Personal Growth Coach, Author, and Editor (Diamond Moments Magazine.) I inspire women to realise their self-worth, find their voice and be rooted in who they are. I offer a safe space where women can take time to get to know themselves intimately, explore their connection to limiting beliefs and break free, becoming more self-aware and using this self-awareness to create the life that they always wanted while feeling supported, understood, and held. The tools I share not only spark new insights but also foster a sense of enthusiasm and connection to self-mastery and ownership of life.

Chapter 14

Val Burgess

From Captivity to Compassion:
Lessons from Leonard Robinson

War profoundly impacts those who endure it. World War II military personnel, especially prisoners of war (POWs), offer us valuable life lessons.

The "*Silent Generation,*" now known as the "Greatest Generation," survived the "Great Depression," a global economic downturn, and fought the most extensive and deadliest military campaign in world history.

Those unlucky to serve in the Pacific relied on their resilience and courage to survive the extreme adversity they experienced in the Pacific theater of war. Allied prisoners quickly understood that as prisoners of Imperial Japan, dying was easier than living.

One of these prisoners, Leonard "Len" L Robinson, fully embraced unconditional forgiveness for his captors. Here is his story:

At Clark Field, located in Luzon in the Philippines, Japanese bombers destroyed this military installation to prevent U.S. interference in their territorial expansion in the Pacific. This second attack began on December 8, 1941, some ten hours after they assaulted Pearl Harbor.

Len dove for this foxhole. While aircraft were ablaze, explosions rocked the earth. Americans died. That day, the Japanese fulfilled their mission and demoralized the American military.

The next day, the United States declared war on Japan.

Originally a draftee, Robinson's service was to be over, and he was to return to the U.S. mainland in just six weeks. However, he then knew he would serve for the duration of the war, however long that was.

As war raged on, Allied soldiers and civilians retreated to the Bataan peninsula, away from the Japanese onslaught on January 7, 1942. By April, nearly everyone in Bataan had one or more diseases: malaria, dengue fever, dysentery, and conditions from malnutrition. With no supplies or support, the U.S. and Filipino soldiers realized their war was over and surrendered on April 9, 1942.

The notorious and lethal Bataan Death March ensued. Some 75,000 Filipinos and Americans were forced to march north 66 miles in stifling hot temperatures. Water and food were withheld. Men were beaten. Some beheaded. Others became roadkill, run over by captured U.S. vehicles. Too many died.

Crammed into sweltering metal rail cars at San Fernando, later, the men marched to Camp O'Donnell, an enclosure surrounded by barbed wire. The camp was filled with sick and dying men. Feces ran down their pant legs. Len moved to the perimeter and rested his legs outside of the wire, avoiding the smell, the sick, and the dying.

Later, Len transferred to Camp Cabanatuan, where he served on the burial detail for a time. Four prisoners carried the deceased in the middle of a large grass mat. Each held the corner of the mat on his shoulder to move the deceased to the communal burial site. They worked in tandem or spilled the body on the ground.

One day, Len, on the front, needed to cross a ditch. He alerted the other carriers, believing they would follow him. They didn't. They stopped. Len fell. The body lay face-to-face with Len. Two days later, he had symptoms of diphtheria, with the bacteria transferred from the deceased POW.

Diphtheria was a lethal disease for starved prisoners. The men were isolated in the "Zero, Zero Ward" as they had zero chance of survival. Len thought he would die. His throat closed. He had paralysis. Death neared. But, little by little, he regained strength.

Five survived, Len included. The benefit for these survivors was that none of the other POWs wanted to be near them. Isolated from the masses, the men healed and cared for one another.

Twenty-four months later, Japan needed laborers. Unmarked freighters, known as Hell Ships, transported thousands of Allied POWs, sometimes for weeks or months and thousands of miles, to occupied territories. Held in the dark, dank, and filthy cargo holds, Len said, "The men endured the horrors of the prison camps magnified tenfold."

Human dignity was destroyed. Fresh air, food, and water were seldom available. Their feces collected in their clothing. Being so thirsty, some drank urine or cut their wrists and drank their own blood. A few resorted to cannibalism. Americans killed Americans while attempting to survive another day on a Hell Ship.

Fourteen of these ships were sunk by Allied torpedoes, killing thousands of prisoners. Allied governments justified these deaths, saying they didn't want the Japanese to know their communication codes had been broken.

Len's ship sailed in September 1943 for Moji, Japan. Once there, the men traveled by train over the mountains and up the western coast to Tokyo 5-B Camp and the port of Niigata. Robinson spent the next twenty-three months working on the docks there.

During the first winter, 25-30 feet of snow fell. The extreme cold hurt their bones. At night, their five rationed blankets failed to keep them warm, as they slept on their wet clothes, attempting to dry them before their next day's work.

Len served as a stevedore and initially moved pig iron into rail cars. Later, he moved all freight. For their labor, they were paid five cents a day.

Their food ration barely sustained them.

At an earlier time, Len studied efficiency in college. He applied that skill to make the prisoner's labor easier. With more efficiency, the guards were rewarded, the workers made more money, and the POWs stood a better chance of survival. Len and the other prisoners soon received an additional bowl of soup. Later, the men received a bag of soybeans, which was placed in the POW's mess (kitchen). While the prisoners grew in strength, they were careful not to show it to save their health.

One day, US aircraft were seen overhead. The men knew their homeland was getting closer.

After nearly two years held at Niigata, the first Allied dive bomber attacked nearby. Then, on August 10, 1945, an all-out battle raged near the stevedores between raiding Allied aircraft and a Japanese destroyer.

The men knew the war soon would be over. In mid August, as they lined up for work, the guards released them, *"the war was over."*

On August 29, two American B-29 Superfortresses dropped numerous 55-gallon drums of food—enough for six meals a day for each of the men. Quickly and carefully, they ate and gained weight.

Leonard Robinson and the other POWs were transported by train on September 5, 1945, to Tokyo. Shocked, they saw a city utterly destroyed.

Staff Sergeant Leonard Robinson, a member of the 200th Coast Artillery Corps, escaped death at least five times during his incarceration. He had faith and always believed he would survive.

Len affirmed that when he left Tokyo, he unconditionally forgave his captives – all of them. He closed the book on that chapter of his life. He recounted that he lived free from trauma and mental health issues throughout his life.

Len shared that he could teach people, especially veterans, how to heal. His method was simple:

- Turn your life over to a higher power. Len gave his to Jesus.
- Be comfortable telling your story, not all the gory details. Yet embrace it all.

- And forgive unconditionally. It is for your health and not those who harmed you.

The day I met Len, he was bent over a bit, relying on his cane to walk up the sidewalk and stairs to his home. As his oral history progressed, his face changed. He looked younger and younger. Len became that young man as he recalled his war. At one point, he jumped out of his chair and hurried down the hallway to retrieve memorabilia to share with me. That evening, he was that young man.

Len's courage and resilience were visible in and through his words. When he spoke of unconditional forgiveness, he shared how it softened him and how he saw his incarceration, thus accepting it.

Len lived with courage and resilience as he served people from many walks of life. His war atrocities gave him the gift of a most directed, giving, and loving existence.

Your capacity for healing from unconditional forgiveness is monumental. By allowing forgiveness, you free yourself from bondage. You build your courage and resilience exponentially. This allows you to embrace your adversity, thus seeing its overall value for your life and your future.

Everything gets bigger and better. Your life expands, your heart warms, and your soul rests as you create a life of your own design. Unconditional forgiveness is true and valuable. I know; it has dramatically changed my life.

Golden Nugget

"The best cure for living a grateful life is to practice unconditional forgiveness for anyone you feel has harmed you!"

About Author:

Name –Val Burgess

Contact – https://www.warsvoices.com

Val Burgess is a World War II POW Historian, Archivist, Educator, and Speaker, dedicated to sharing the inspiring stories of prisoners of war through her platform, Wars' Voices. Val has documented these narratives for over three decades, enriched her life, and offered profound life lessons. These stories highlight courage, resilience, and unconditional forgiveness, guiding us toward personal liberation. Val believes that we can overcome past grievances and self-imposed limitations, leading us to a life of joy, freedom, and fulfillment. Join Val on this transformative journey and discover the keys to unlocking your best life.

Chapter 15

LS Kirkpatrick
My Four Super Powers

You see, it was my grandchildren who started me with the writing process because I wrote them stories. Then my daughter said you've got to get this book out for everyone else, so one thing led to another, and here I am, 24 books later.

I'm LS Kirkpatrick, a multiple award-winning international bestselling author who will be working on more books before the end of the year. I help people express the value they have inside themselves to the world. That's through finding their purpose in writing a book or acting on their purpose in other ways, like entrepreneurship.

The first children's book I wrote is Riding Frogs in the Backyard. This one I wrote for my two granddaughters, who were four and six at the time. We were outside playing with frogs. Their dad would bring home pollywogs, aka tadpoles, from the little puddles at work, and the girls got to watch them grow into frogs. I wanted to write a book about them having fun outside, and that's how this book started. The illustrations are just amazing. My daughter's childhood friend is an illustrator, and she does amazing artwork. She asked me to please not ask her to do this again because it's not her style, but she did this for my daughter, and I'm so thankful to Hannah Falanga for doing that.

When we first moved to Texas, we were looking for a place to live, and we went to this town called Hutto. There are concrete hippos everywhere in this town, and I wondered what is up with all these hippos? Well, we went into a restaurant called the Hippo Cafe, and there they had this giant mural of a hippo and a second giant mural of a hippo with a train, and I thought I had to write this story.

So, I just started writing the story and had it done by the time we finished lunch. That night, I wondered what the real story was, so I looked it up, and I was only off by a couple of things. I changed those and came up with the book Henrietta: the Hutto Hippo. I got it to be an Amazon number one bestseller, which really started my publishing career. I guess that is when I acknowledged my Writing Superpower.

I also did something very different, as I have the original story in it, and I also have all the concrete hippos with the actual website that says where all of those hippos are. I included more information about the town. They have an annual hippo day, and every Friday, they show their school spirit by wearing orange. There is a large mural that was painted on an outside wall of one of the buildings in town, and I talked about that and showed pictures of it. Of course, I had to put the Hippo Cafe in it because that's where I wrote the story. It also shows that the trains are still running there in the town. There's more to this book than just the story itself, and it was so much fun.

After this book, I decided children needed to write their own stories, which is why I came up with The One and Only Write Your Own Story book. In it, I guide children on how to write their own stories. There are blank pages where they can write their stories and put in pictures if they want to.

At the end, I wrote, "What do you do if someone makes fun of your story or if someone says they don't like your story." I let the readers know that it is okay because not every story is for everyone. Many authors have stories that some people like and other people do not like. What is wonderful is that you wrote your story the way you imagined it or remembered it, and that is what is important. (That goes for adults, too.)

I have another story that I'm still working on. I mean, I have it finished; I have it in a book, but I don't like the beginning of it. That sometimes happens with authors, but if you can see this beautiful child here with this beautiful puppy on the cover, that's my granddaughter, and this is my Irish Wolfhound puppy. She was able to hold it and take care of it before I was even able to see it.

It has not been an easy journey, but to really have a dream and pursue it. I started to get into the world of owning my own business and being an entrepreneur, and the doors just burst wide open. There is this whole world I didn't even know existed.

I didn't know who Tony Robbins was; I saw him in a movie one time, and that was it. I really didn't know who he was. I didn't know who Les Brown was, didn't know who James Malinchak or John Tarico were. I didn't even know a lot of the authors; it just wasn't anything that I had been a part of before. Now I've met so many people, and I have my own live show, which is on every Friday and then on TV on Saturday.

I was able to go to New York City by myself; I never thought I'd ever do anything like that. And part of that thinking was because - that was for other people, not me - I grew up with that because that's the way my parents thought. Now I thought, why aren't they for us, why not me? These are things that I would love to do! One thing I want to do is play piano at Carnegie Hall in New York. I'm setting things in motion to do that, and it was and still is a mindset.

Two years ago, I learned that the subconscious controls the conscious mind. You know, all those negative things put into your brain that tell you can't, you're not good enough, you're not worthy. That was a belief I grew up with. I always felt I was not worthy, and it was all a lie.

The Legacy that I want to leave with my grandchildren is that they are worthy and that they can do what they want to do. Dreaming big and going after those dreams, and by achieving my dreams by going after them, I've set a precedent for them, and they're actually proud of me. They talk about me and my books, and it just fills my heart because I want them to know that they're more.

Do what you can do, and don't be afraid to step out. I look at fear as a hologram; we know that a hologram looks real and can do amazing things, but it's not real. You can put your hand through it; it's not there. You can step through it. It's not there, so look at fear as a hologram - it's just there, but it's not real, and so you step through it. You take that first step to something you want to do, and don't let fear hold you back.

You know, I've heard the phrase that there's one place that is full of dreams and visions that people have, and it's called a cemetery because they never did anything with those dreams and visions. They stay there, and once they are there, you can't get them back.

So, do it now; you're not too old, you're not too young, and if you find somebody who is doing something that you want to do (and you will), you learn from them. It's okay if a hundred other people are doing it because, like I said before, you are unique, and the way you think about things and the way you're going to do things is going to be different than those other hundred people.

Don't let that intimidate you. Don't think that you are never going to be as good because you're right, you're not, you're going to be different, and you're going to be the best you are out there. That's going to be better in that respect, so don't compare yourself to others. That's a big trap, a big, big trap, and it's a trap that takes you nowhere. That is their journey, not yours; learn from what they did and bring it into your journey, and then go on. We're all here to help each other.

When I was younger, I believed that you went and got a job with good benefits and that was all you needed to do, but that is not so and hasn't been for many years. When I was young and my children were young, I felt like I was not doing a good job because there was so much to juggle, and when I worked out of the home for someone else, there was even more to do. My show starts with: Are you wondering if this is all there is to life? Wasn't I meant to do something more? Isn't there something more out there than what I'm doing? The answer is yes.

If you feel that way, then there definitely is something else out there for you. The biggest thing is don't quit, don't quit, don't quit, but you can pause. Pause is a really good thing. Pause means you're taking time to reflect on what's going on; you're taking time to assess the situation, but don't ever quit. It's so easy to quit.

I told a young friend of mine who was helping us out on the farm a few years ago; he hated, I mean, he really hated his full-time job, and I said, "Whatever you do, don't quit while you hate your job." He looked at me like, "What are you talking about," and he asked me.

I said that this is the advice I was given: "If you quit while you hate your job, it's never going to improve; you're always going to quit when things are tough. If you stick with it and you quit when things are really good, then you know you wanted to quit for a good reason, not just because it got tough."

Now, for him, the situation he was in, it just never got better, but he assessed it at that point, and it's like, am I having a tough time just because I'm going through a tough time right now and I'm learning, and I'm growing? Or is it a tough time because this is a toxic thing, and it's really not good for me? He decided on whether to stay or not for him.

He left and found another job that he absolutely loved. If it's toxic, get rid of it because it's not doing you or anybody any good. If it's just you're having a bad day, that could be that you're growing. If you feel that you have failed, say I've been doing this, and I keep doing it wrong, and I keep doing it wrong, well, that's good because you're finding out things that are not working so you can keep working to find the thing that does work. It sounds crazy, but don't quit because it's tough. I've wanted to quit, and if I had, I would never would have been able to go, do, or be where I am right now.

I wouldn't be here to encourage you to keep going if I wasn't doing these things myself. That is my second superpower. Letting my Light Shine. You need to have the support and the help you need. Someone asked who the top five people are that you're around. Are they encouraging? If the people you're around the most are not encouraging you, you need to be around other people who are encouraging, who are supporting, and who are helping you. I had to distance myself from a couple of family members because as much as I do love them, they were not helping me.

Sometimes, other people have a limit on what they can dream and what they can imagine. Their limit may be right here, and your level may be up here. I think John Maxwell calls it the "cap," but if they can't get past this level and they're holding you down, you just need to distance yourself so you can get up to the level you want to be.

That is okay; you're not getting rid of them, and you're not saying goodbye forever. What you are doing is getting yourself where you want to be; the family loves you, but sometimes they can't see your vision, and they can't see the way you see it.

A family member told my daughter, "That's just a pipe dream." Who cares? It's her dream. If she wants to go for it, let her; if she makes a success out of it, amazing! If she didn't, at least she tried to go for it and see what she could do. She's doing great; she hasn't stopped.

Life gets in the way, and that's the other thing you're always going to have. Distractions. You need to make sure they don't prevent you from going where you're going. Distractions are going to happen; prepare for them, but keep going. That's the big thing right there: don't quit.

That's my third Superpower, the Superpower of Perseverance. Walking through fear, taking the risk to get the great reward it offers, and not quitting when things get really tough, and they do get really tough, being a great cheerleader for others to help them reach their dreams.

I have programs/courses on my website, and one of them is called Finding Your Me. It's helping you find your purpose. What is it that really excites you and really lights you up? Then, we go on to act upon that purpose. Okay, now you know what you really want to do, what you really love to do, and how you continue from there, so we go on with that.

It's a wonderful journey! If I hadn't written that book to my granddaughters, if I hadn't listened to my daughter saying you got to get this published, if I wouldn't have done this, then I wouldn't be where I am now. I would not have my own TV show. I mean, I never thought of myself doing that, but I love it. I love it because I bring value to people and enrich their lives, and that's what I want to do.

I want to encourage you, enrich your life, and help you live a better life. That's what I want to leave with my grandchildren and my great-grandchildren: to keep passing on the message, not to believe the lies and things you've been told but to go after what you want to do. To be the best you, and every day, we're a little bit better than we were yesterday. I love it, I love it so.

The gold nugget that I share all the time, and I will keep sharing, is this: You are valuable, you are worthy, you are enough, and you matter. Why? Because it's very true! There's no one else like you; there will never be anyone else like you because only you have made the choices you have made, and that makes you so unique that only you can give what nobody else in the world can give. That's what the world wants to hear; they want to know about you.

It seems that is my fourth Superpower: helping you find your value inside of you. It is that value in you that is your worth, not your job or what is outside of you. Your value and your worth are what makes you enough, and all of that is why you do matter in this world, this universe. You matter. You have a voice, and the world is waiting to hear.

Golden Nugget

"You have great value, You are worthy,
You are enough, and You do matter.'

About Author:

Name – LS Kirkpatrick

Contact –https://www.LSKirkpatrick.com

LS Kirkpatrick is a multiple Award-winning International Bestselling Author, International Speaker, Guiding Life Coach, a dynamo TV host of the "Value In You" show, mentor, editor and publisher, editor in chief of the Wisdom on the Front Porch magazine, and founder of the Orphan and Widows not-for-profit foundation. She is also a loving wife, caring mother of 4, and energetic grandmother to 15 grandchildren. She guides others to write, publish and achieve their dreams, their vision of success. Her main mission is to guide others to "See the value in yourself and live your purpose with courage". LS absolutely loves all that she does.

Chapter 16

Angel Marie Monachelli

Ignite Your Ultimate Energy, Joy, and Abundance

Do you ever feel like success is just out of reach, obscured by countless obstacles blocking your path? Have you ever felt low Energy and extreme pain in your whole body? Does it seem like no matter what you do, there's always something stopping you from feeling great and being successful?

If these questions resonate with you, then you're not alone. Let me share a secret with you — in those moments of darkness, when it feels like all hope is lost, there is still a glimmer of light waiting to guide you. It may come in unexpected forms, like the touch of a massage therapist's hands or the gentle Energy of Reiki healing.

Like so many of you, I carried the weight of emotional wounds inflicted during childhood, compounded by the spiritual condemnation of a faith system that failed to provide comfort. I constantly feared persecution merely for being true to myself and loving honestly in a world that still struggles to embrace diversity.

For years, I sought refuge by numbing the pain, convinced it was the sole means of escaping the torment that loomed over me. Yet, in numbing the pain, I gradually realized I was also dimming my vibrant, brilliant light. And that, my friend, is simply unacceptable.

I remember vividly the first time I felt the sharp jab of needles piercing my fingers, a sensation so intense it reverberated through every fiber of my being. Holding my little one's hand tightly as we crossed the street, a deep fear gripped me. I felt like I might never feel the simple joy of holding her hand, or anyone else's, ever again. It was like a knife cutting through my heart, leaving me broken. Then, at a speaking engagement, the mic made a horrific squealing sound, and suddenly, my whole nervous system shivered, and my body seized up with extreme pain. At that moment, I feared that I would never be able to speak on stage again.

Living with lupus, fibromyalgia, arthritis, Sjogren's, and several other diseases with long names means the mere acts of being touched, standing up, walking, or even breathing caused immense discomfort. Amazingly, amidst the daily reality of relentless pain, my adventure has been one of resilience and joy ever since I discovered how to ignite my healing Energy.

My dear friend, have you ever found yourself facing a moment that felt like the end of everything you knew? A moment where fear gripped your heart so tightly that you questioned whether you could ever move forward again?

I understand the paralyzing fear that grips you, the uncertainty that clouds your mind, leaving you wondering, "What now? What do I DO?" When that perfect storm created my breaking point, it was my breakthrough point. I realized I had to figure it out; I had to do something. Research from four decades ago suggested that massage helps with stress and pain, leaving me convinced it was my best option, so I hired a massage therapist.

Yes, I was skeptical at first. Raised in a background where such practices seemed foreign, I hesitated. Yet desperation often opens doors we never thought possible; however, this wasn't the quick fix I expected. When my therapist started the massage, my skin suddenly felt like it was going to burst open! The intense irritation of the pain made me scream, "Stop! Stop touching me! You're hurting me!" Even after she stopped, my skin was on fire!

With what felt like divine inspiration, she offered an alternative: Reiki Energy Healing. I said, "I come from a Catholic and

Christian background. I'm not sure that you can heal me with Energy." She asked me to take a deep breath. I did. I remember while taking that breath, I thought, "What the heck? I'll try anything to make this pain stop!" So I said, "Go for it!" And so, with a leap of faith and trust, I embraced the healing power of Reiki.

OMG! I must tell you -- within 10 seconds, I felt 'ENERGY' move through me. The vibration was so soothing, and I felt so connected. The pain dropped from a seven to a four just like that. I remember thinking, "Wow! This Energy stuff is real, and it heals!"

Even though the buzzing nerve pain in my body wasn't totally gone, I felt a calmness come over me. This subtle touch was my first glimpse of hope and relief. From that moment, I dove in headfirst, ready to share the power of Reiki Energy Healing with the world.

My first step was to learn everything I possibly could about Reiki Healing Energy and the understanding of Quantum Physics about Energy. Back then, over two decades ago, it was not easy because the practice of Energy work and the science behind it was an emerging art surrounded by general skepticism.

Despite the cultural obstacles, I persevered and attained the Reiki Master/Teacher level. Reiki has given me a process for relaxation and a system that helps me to stay in alignment with my true purpose every day. Alleviating the physical pain allowed me to breathe. As I regained my personal shine, I started the discovery process of learning about the power of Energy. I discovered the power of Mindset and the power of nurturing the Headset, Heartset, and Gutset.

Because this is real life, it's not the end of my story. Once I got the pain to a manageable place, I discovered that the emotional and spiritual trauma and pain had expanded. And that, my friend, was no longer acceptable! So, I put my intention into nurturing and accepting my feelings. Wow! For a Gemini, it was not fun!

Having cultivated the skills and mindset required to flow with the obstacles, I now run a successful spiritual counseling business. My journey has led me to become a ten-time international best-selling author and the producer and host of multiple TV shows. I sustain the high Energy that my life commitment demands by tapping into the infinite Energy of the universe.

I feel so blessed because, along the adventure of learning Reiki, I learned about the healing power of breathing. Yeah, I know, we all breathe. What I learned was a deep diaphragmatic breathing technique that brings oxygen to every cell, including those in the brain. What this does is plump up the cells with oxygen, which they need for ultimate wellness. Physically, this streamlines your thinking, releases hormones to calm you, and triggers your muscles to activate, making you feel more Energetic.

Deep diaphragmatic breathing also clarifies the thinking process. It calms the body and mind so that I can really connect to my soul's consciousness. Breathing has been essential to my physical, emotional, and spiritual healing, and now it is a non-negotiable part of my daily self-care routine.

Embracing Reiki wasn't just about alleviating physical pain; it was about embarking on a journey of self-discovery and healing. It taught me to breathe deeply, drawing in the very essence of life itself. With each breath, I felt my cells awaken, my thoughts clarified, and my spirit soaring.

So let's play and raise our consciousness and breathe together. I am known as the "Breath Pusher!" Take a deep breath. Feel the Energy flowing through you and know that you are not alone. Together, we will rise, stronger and more resilient than ever before.

Plus, this is not the end of the story; it is the beginning of a journey filled with healing, joy, and infinite Energy possibilities.

Let's Do It Now! Starting at the top, visualize your breath with gentle waves of healing Energy through your head. Clearing out all the clutter, distractions, and shiny objects. When my Headset has clarity, I feel a subtle tingling that starts in the middle of my forehead and moves to the temples, then down the sides of my neck and to my shoulders.

That's me. What do you feel? In the beginning, it could be subtle. As you continue to practice and pay attention to your deep breathing practice, you will notice more sensations. It could feel like a tingling scalp or other tingling; goosebumps; calm; the inner dialog stops pestering you; a sense of "Oh, I get it now! And I feel it now!" Stop now and notice for yourself: what does it feel like when you have clarity in your Headset?

Continuing through the process of breathing, move your attention to your Heartset, your innermost desires, and your guiding values. Breathe into your heart, clearing out all the junk of anger, frustration, and fear and replacing it all with love: love for yourself exactly as you are right now, love for others, and love for who you are meant to be. Tap into that love and feel honored for your values. Lovingly accept yourself and your passion and purpose.

Continuing through the breathing process, move your attention to your Gutset, which refers to our instinctual understanding, often manifested as gut feelings. Despite popular belief, intuition is a subconscious process drawing from past observations. It guides us toward what's important and what to ignore, though it doesn't always yield clear answers.

Balancing gutset with heartset and headset prevents impulsive actions. It ensures that our choices are aligned with long-term goals and our higher self. Harmoniously integrating these three elements enhances decision-making. You choose your path with grace, ease, and glory for who you are!

I encourage you to practice breathing techniques throughout the day. For example, at every red light, take three deep diaphragmatic breaths.And my friend, contact me and share how you feel.

What is my superpower? Wisdom from one of my Reiki Students:

"I knew the first time I met you, Angel, that I wanted to know more about what you do. I already knew about Reiki and Energy work, but I had never heard of the term Lightworker. During our first session of spiritual counseling and Reiki clearing, I understood that I was on the right path. I was ecstatic! I had found my teacher! You gave me techniques to continue clearing and energizing myself and all the spaces I encounter, as well as the water I drink and the food I serve and eat. And you gave me a powerful breathing practice that anyone can do for more Energy, joy, and abundance. I was months into recovery after a tough surgery. As we regularly continued to meet, my recovery accelerated. I started seeing even bigger changes when I started doing weekly Tai Chi with you. I stopped taking maximum doses of pain meds every day, my balance and coordination improved, and my intuition grew by magnitudes. You helped me reawaken my natural ability to see and feel Energy. You helped me step into my power to help others heal and experience joy every day. When I read your Spiritual Cookbook, I experienced a review of everything you taught me. I felt elevated and connected to universal life force Energy, my personal Shining Wheel, my favorite crystals, and my spirit guide animals. I am so honored to be your Reiki student. Your continuous support, Reiki Share, and spiritual counseling, and especially your friendship, bring joy to my life."

For over 30 years, I have been honored and blessed by every one of my students, and I gracefully step into my superpower to help others ignite their gifts and healing Energy. In addition, I have another cool superpower where I can help people feel their energetic field, the "ENERGY" all around them! It's a unique ability that people have told me they can feel: My light, and it looks like I'm glowing.

I do this at significant events, such as conferences and summits, both online and in person. It's not just about thinking about the feeling – it's about feeling, really feeling the feeling. It affects you as though you are waking up to a whole new world of feelings you never had before. I would love to have the fun of helping you step into your superhero vibes because igniting happiness and good feelings wherever I go is so nurturing to others and part of my soul's commitment to the world.

As I conclude this beautiful conversation, my soul's commitment to the world persists. I believe in your ability to create positive Energy, shape your present moment, and cultivate a joyous, abundant life. If these words have sparked something within you, and if you're drawn to reach out and go deeper, do it now! Let's keep sharing this incredible path to fulfillment together. Thank you for joining me, embracing your gifts, and contributing your Energy and light to the world.

Dear friend, may your adventures be limitless!

Golden Nugget

"Change your Mindset, Ignite your ENERGY and Shine On!"

About Author:

Name – Angel Marie Monachelli

Contact – https://angelmarieinc.com/

Angel Marie is a multi-gifted beacon of inspiration and transformation. As a TV Producer & Host, she infuses positive Energy into stories and empowers others through the incredible realms of Energy and Healing. She's not just an author; she's a 10-time International Best-Selling Author, sharing her wisdom, knowledge and insights with readers worldwide. As the Executive VP for On the Marc TV, she helps you stream your brand to the world.

As a Certified Spiritual Counselor, she has been a guiding light for countless souls on their journey to self-discovery, helping them experience their Energy, ignite their true gifts, and create greater abundance. With deep gratitude and over 25 years of Reiki Mastery, she shines as a radiant beacon of love and healing, touching lives with her profound compassion, joy and wisdom.

Chapter 17

Dr. Alexandra McDermott and Jae Wilcox

How a Mother and Daughter Combine to Create the S.O.U.L. of a Diamond

We have both shared stories that have referenced each other, but this time, we decided, why not finally write a story together? Our intention in writing this story is quite simple: share with others how to create and sustain a similar connection to our open and soul-deep relationship as mother and daughter.

Undoubtedly, it is a difficult task that requires work, balance, and understanding. Thus, we wanted to share our journey and how we turned our relationship into a Diamond.

What We Can Learn from the Strength of a Diamond

When you think of a Diamond, you think of strong, beautiful, and maybe even raw.

While we immediately think of a Diamond as a gemstone and a flashy piece in our jewelry, its true identity is merely a mineral. A Diamond is composed of the same element that flows through every life form. Much like fingerprints, Diamonds are unique. No two are alike. They are naturally flawed, found in nature battered and polished by the elements over the years. They have a "lived" experience. While they are not sentient, they have a soul.

Diamonds can withstand almost anything; even though they crack, they crack into smaller Diamonds. When we think about our relationship as mother and daughter, we compare it to a Diamond. Throughout the ups and downs of life, throughout the cracks, our relationship remains dazzling.

Our mantra has always been "I love you to the core of my being" – no words, no temporary actions or behaviors could ever damage that truth. We believe the secret to our connection is our mutual honesty, support for each other, and willingness to communicate our feelings. It takes true bravery to be as open and honest as we have been with each other. Over the years, there have been many times when not-so-positive things must be shared between one another, and it has taken a lot of courage. But we do it anyway, regardless of the discomfort, awkwardness, or tension. With the right intention, when done out of love, it strengthens your bond and doesn't harm it.

S — therefore, stands for Strength.

Managing Difficult Relationships, Creating Boundaries, Protecting Your Energy, and Asking for Support

O—stands for Outlast. According to Merriam's Dictionary, outlast is a verb that means "to last longer than, to continue to exist, and be active" longer than someone or something. In our case, we need to serve as pillars of strength for each other first and ensure that when we encounter challenges, we step up for each other, and one of us can pull the other through when we cannot see the other side.

In every relationship, there are bound to be tough conversations that need to be had. Often, people avoid these awkward and nerve-wracking conversations. However, with the right intention and environment, once the conversation ends, there is nothing but love and support for one another. It requires uncomfortable honesty, understanding (in all aspects), and unconditional love and support. That means support in all forms: esteem, tangible, informational, and emotional.

Throughout many relationships in both of our lives, we have noticed that support is usually where people fall short. It is hard to ask for support. It takes a lot of courage. You feel like you may be placing an unnecessary or unwanted burden on another person. However, through many conversations, we realize we can't read each other's minds, although that would be entertaining at times. To get support, you need to ask for it.

For example, for years, as a mother, I have been trying to get to the root cause of medical symptoms I cannot explain, from my head to my toes – I can give you a laundry list here of strange things. To me, now, it is merely a list. However, Jae insists on being with me for many doctor's appointments. She has been my only constant. She has helped me maintain my positive mindset when things have become increasingly complex, and when things are challenging for her, I have also been able to do the same for her. Sometimes, I felt I should not ask for her support, but I knew I needed her, and she was glad she was there for me. I could not imagine the appointments if she wasn't there, and she felt the same way.

It is easy to show up for people, especially people you love. Encouragement, reminding people of their strengths, and celebrating successes are easy ways to give esteem support. Showing up, going to those appointments, and being there physically is tangible support in such a simple form.

We have always told each other that we need to examine the people around us to ensure they support what we want to achieve. If they are not, we need to make the necessary changes to create space for those who are. We must also understand how to protect our energy, design, build, and sustain healthy relationships, and manage boundaries.

At times, each of us has been engaged in unhealthy or toxic relationships with other people. This has required one of us to have an honest conversation about the impact of this relationship and what kind of support we could provide. We provided informational support by facing each other with the reality of what was happening and ensuring we knew all the information. We helped each other leave the situation and physically and emotionally supported each other before, during, and after the departure. We went through the stages of grief, but not alone, together.

U — stands for Understanding.

To create a strong bond, we must understand what we are going through at different points in each other's lives. To do that, however, we must remain engaged with each other. Our relationship cannot just be a transactional one. It must be a full and loving relationship where we know about each other's lives, are present regardless of where we live, and deeply understand what the other person is going through at that point in their life.

Reframing the Typical "Mother-Daughter" Fights

We would never want to paint our relationship as perfect, although we love what we have and cherish our relationship. Every mother-daughter relationship has those ridiculously petty fights that you laugh about years later but can be genuinely appalling at the moment. One thing we can and will share, though, is that we never let fights linger. It is easy to lose track of what a fight is about when there is pure emotion involved, but once all the cards are dealt and all things are done and said, we always find a way to crack a joke. Humor is our love language. We both know that whatever it is we're fighting about – it's not that serious. It doesn't change our love for one another or the strength of our relationship. That love deepens our relationship, friendship, and bond.

L — stands for Love.

Ways to Create a Resilient Relationship Like a Diamond

Tragically, we both have dealt with many crises throughout our lives. Amid our serial crises, we knew we always had a choice: show up or don't.

One thing remains clear: as mother and daughter, we always choose the same thing: *show up*. This requires diamond-like resilience.

Resilience is defined as the ability to bounce back quickly and withstand difficult events. It can be taught and learned. Being resilient doesn't mean things won't bother or hurt you. It means you can handle things thrown at you more easily, and they won't knock you down or keep you down.

A recent article by the Mayo Clinic does an excellent job listing ways to strengthen your resilience: "Resilience: Build Skills to Endure Hardship." In summary, it says that to improve your resilience, you should build strong, healthy relationships; do something purposeful every day; journal about past events and learn from them; remain hopeful; actively support your well-being through diet, exercise, mindfulness, etc. and take action to improve your life. Don't ignore your challenges.

In our case, strengthening our relationship every day is a priority for us. This requires work and energy on our part. We now live in separate states, but communicate in some way every day, whether via text, phone, video chat, or just by sending a meme to each other. The bottom line is we check in, and by doing that, we say: I love you, I see you, I miss you, and I am here for you.

Our Wish for You

We are all blessed to live in a highly connected world where we can share our experiences. We are honored to be able to share ours with you. Each day, you can show up in the world – how you wish to be – and we hope you show up as the S.O.U.L. of a diamond. We want you to be able to create deep, soul-inspired connections in your life with people who align with your values and support your vision for the beautiful life you build with intention and purpose. You control your joy.

Golden Nugget
To Make Tomorrow More Joyful than Today

Author Name:
Name – Dr. Alexandra McDermott and Jae Wilcox
Contact – (12) Alexandra McDermott, JD, MFA, EdD | LinkedIn

I'm Dr. Alexandra "Ali" McDermott. I am a global advocate with over 25 years of experience in various fields, including writing, law, education, entrepreneurship, research, health, and dogs.

I am passionate about advocating for the collaboration, innovation, creativity, and well-being of people worldwide.

Through multiple platforms, I aim to help people create the life of their dreams with intention.

I am the CEO/Founder of Pen Crown Publishing and McDermott Leadership. We help people share their messages with high impact and leave the legacy they wish to leave in the world.

Chapter 18

Christine Jaya Williamson

The Secret Scared Garden Space

Do you have that space in your life? Maybe it's a closet, a drawer, a room, a location you avoid because it's a throw zone for anything you don't want to deal with. You tell yourself you will deal with it later, when you have the time, or when you feel that zap of motivation that just doesn't come. Or maybe it's a symbolic space deep inside, born out of physical, mental, or emotional pain.

In the story I'm about to share, it was a place inside my heart that led to a feeling that I just don't matter or belong - even after years of working through and healing trauma, abuse, and other mental and emotional struggles of hurt, pain, and shame. This place in my heart felt like an abandoned cave that was dark, dismal, haunted, and tortured, and I knew it needed my attention.

I'm no stranger to facing tough challenges. I had an abusive childhood; I was sexually and physically assaulted, developed an eating disorder, battled and overcame postpartum depression, and then a psychosis. Our youngest daughter is a multi-diagnosed, special needs (now adult) child with significant and challenging around-the-clock care requirements. I initially dove headfirst into being a mom and wife, giving it everything until my body, mind, and spirit broke, leaving me in the fight of my life. Ultimately, I triumphed, and through that experience, I knew I was born to support other moms in navigating their challenges, looking after their families, and including themselves in the care and nurturing they offer to others.

Being an Empowered Mom means having the skills, strategies, and ability to create pathways of possibilities, no matter how challenging it may seem in the moment. In the heart of every journey lies the courage to face the shadows and find the light within. For me, that journey began in the depths of a cave, not of stone, but of emotions and memories long buried. It was a place I had avoided for years, a dark chamber of hurt and pain that I hadn't dared to explore. What I had figured out was that I needed to learn how to nurture myself - something that had never come naturally to me.

When I realized that there was still a place inside me that needed attention, and I couldn't navigate it on my own, I asked for help. I felt a mixture of fear and curiosity tugging at my heart. With the gentle encouragement of my therapist, I took the first step into the unknown.

I was scared, I'm not going to lie. I didn't know what to expect. I knew this place was created by remnants of feelings of being invisible, not enough, and that I was "bad." Even with all the forgiveness, love, and acceptance that I had extended to myself and others, there was this part of me that I hadn't yet acknowledged. I'm not even sure of the reason other than it was still painful. I felt shame rising when I thought about all the work I had already done and the fact that I still needed help to face something.

Yet, as I stood at the entrance of that cavernous space within me, I felt a mixture of fear and curiosity tugging at my heart. With the gentle encouragement of my therapist, I closed my eyes and took the next step into the unknown. She said, "What if you opened your ears and listened? What do you hear?" I could hear water. I love water. "What else do you hear?" she asked.

Silence. It wasn't scary, though; it was almost comforting. The darkness enveloped me like a heavy blanket. She then invited me to open my eyes, use the light, and look around. And as my eyes adjusted, I began to see something unexpected. It was a living garden wall, vibrant and breathing with life.

Mosses and vines cascaded down its surface while delicate flowers bloomed in every hue imaginable. Cool water was dripping down the wall, giving life to it all. The thing was, it wasn't just any garden; it was a manifestation of my inner world, a reflection of the beauty that lay hidden within my soul. As I looked about, I saw a garden bench with a plaque on it. What does it say, I wonder? A little girl was sitting on the bench looking at something in her hand, but it was too dark for her to see it. Wait! I have a light, maybe I can help her!

The little girl looked familiar. Where had I seen her before? As I made my way over to the bench, she looked up at me and said, "I was waiting for someone like you to come. I got lost here a long time ago, and I had no one to help me. I found this, and I think it's a rock, but it's too dark to tell."

I asked her name, and she said it was Christine. "I love your name. That's my name, too," I told her. And then it came to me: she was a mirror of my past self, lost and alone in the darkness.

As I used my light to look at the rock, she had this undeniable sparkle in her eyes. I remembered that sparkle. I felt it wash over me the way the water on the garden wall brought nourishment to the plants. What she held in her hand wasn't just a rock; it was a sparkling rose quartz – a symbol of love and healing and a reminder that even in the darkest of times, there is beauty to be found.

It was stunning! I asked her where she found it, and she pointed behind us. I asked her to show me, and she took my hand and guided me while I used my light. I could see the ground and walls covered in rose quartz, clear quartz, diamonds, and other empowering crystals that sparkled like stars in the night sky. Each one held a unique significance, from the strength of diamonds forged under pressure to the clarity of quartz guiding the way forward.

It was breathtaking. She said, "WOW, I have never been able to see fully in the cave before. I could feel things shifting and changing, so I am so glad you found me so I could finally see what was all around me. All I had was this bench, and I could hear the water. I love water." "Me too," I said.

She told me she had carved a message to herself, and I softly whispered, "To us, sweet child," on that bench. The message was: "Christine, I see you even in the dark and when you are alone. One day, others will see you, too. And what a treasure that will be."

I felt it. I could start to embody it, a promise to never forget the light that exists within, even in our darkest moments. And as I traced the words with my fingers, I felt a sense of peace wash over me. It started to come together for me at that moment.

That child was truly me, a part of me that was still isolated and alone. This place wasn't just a dark, abandoned cave; it was a Secret Sacred Garden Space, created for me by me, filled with all the values, life-giving energy, love, and creation - and now to be filled with joy as well.

I can now cultivate courage, integrating bravery to build trust, inviting healing and transformation through optimism and acceptance, laying a foundation of understanding, love, and joy, and building a bridge to peace. This transformation is not only for me as I continue on my journey but for all of humanity, being a beacon of hope that no matter what we are facing, there are pathways of possibilities. Staying curious and connected, using empathy and compassion to be that light in someone else's darkness.

What does it mean to self-nurture? Along my journey, I have learned how to see, value, accept, love, and befriend myself. I even found ways to give myself self-care along the way. So when this idea of self-nurturing came to my awareness, I was once again on a journey of discovering something new.

When I had my children, I had to learn how to nurture them - it wasn't something that came naturally. I didn't know how, so I read books, watched shows, and asked my therapist. Over the years, I learned how to "manufacture" nurture, and I became pretty good at it, while at the same time, I didn't actually understand how.

Discovering my Secret Sacred Garden Space, along with other skills and strategies I have learned along the way, I learned what self-nurturing is and how to cultivate it within myself instead of it being manufactured outside of me. While it is like self-care, the art of self-nurturing is being able to really identify what you need, want, and yearn for, and then deciding that you are worthy of those things, practicing how to give them to yourself and using self-care as a way to deliver the nurturing. The secret is allowing and accepting the gift of receiving.

In this sacred garden space, I found not only healing but transformation and a newfound sense of purpose. It was a place where I could cultivate courage, embrace vulnerability, and build bridges of empathy and compassion. As I journeyed back to the surface, I carried with me the knowledge that no matter what challenges lay ahead, I would always have a sanctuary within me—a beacon of hope to guide me on my path to healing and wholeness.

We are all unique, and each of us will have our own experience on the path to healing. If you have your own deep and hidden wounds, I'd like to offer a gentle and heartfelt piece of advice: don't wait too long to step on the path to healing. The only thing more difficult and painful than mustering the courage to ask for help, face and release our wounds is not doing it. Just take that first step, and then the next... There is a sacred space in every one of us. Go claim yours

Golden Nugget

"I am a creator of pathways of unlimited possibilities no matter how challenging things may seem in the given moment."

About Author:

Name – Christine Jaya Williamson
Contact – https://mybeaconofhopecoach.com/

Christine is a dedicated professional with a wealth of experience and expertise in guiding individuals towards empowerment, resilience, and fulfillment. With a background as a certified Emotional Intelligence coach and tutor, Christine has devoted significant time and energy to supporting others in navigating life's challenges and unlocking their true potential. She has received her Coaching Certification from the Institute of Women Centered Coaching, Training, and Leadership and is currently studying Facilitation. Through this training Christine founded her Beacon Of Hope Heart Centered Coaching Business, providing a compassionate and supportive space for overwhelmed moms to find balance and empowerment in their lives.

Chapter 19

Marie Bailey
From Sorrow to Sunshine

"Sometimes," said Pooh, "The smallest things take up the most room in your heart" – A.A. Milne.

The little girl watched as her big, strong daddy brought the little fancy white box into the house and took it to the parlor, and she just knew what it was! "Only beautiful Baby Dolls came in beautiful white boxes," and she knew she just knew that this was her baby doll! She knew by how carefully he carried the box in his strong hands; she always loved his strong, gentle hands, and he was so careful not to drop such a precious gift. The excitement and anticipation were building.

She hung around the door waiting for her dad to come out, and when he did, he closed the door, took her hand, and led her to the kitchen, telling her that she was not to go into the room. Being that "she knew what she knew" and being a very inquisitive child, her dad left the house, and she headed for the room. Her mom was in her room resting, and her grandmother was with her, and there was no one else around. The coast was clear! She just wanted to take a quick peek at her baby doll; no one would know!

She sneaked into the room and climbed up onto the chair next to the table where the beautiful box was sitting. She was careful not to kneel on her favorite red dress and get it wrinkled. She was not sure why she had to wear her best dress when it was not even Sunday, but her grandma had said she should. She looked around to make sure no one was coming, and then she lifted the lid just a little to take a quick peek.

The baby doll was dressed in a beautiful white dress. She was perfect, with a beautiful glow around her. She had the face of a sleeping angel, which was what she had always imagined angels looked like. She decided right then and there that she loved this baby doll and that she was going to love her forever. She started to lift the lid a bit more when her dad and grandmother came into the room.

Her dad lifted her gently to the floor, and her grandmother took her by the hand and led her from the room, leaving her dad inside. She was probably in trouble; she often was. She could not understand why her dad had tears in his eyes, her big, strong dad, and her grandmother was also softly crying. She had never seen her dad cry before, and she hoped that she had not made them cry. She walked to her mom's bedroom, listened at the door, and heard her softly crying inside! She had only wanted to peek and did not think it was that bad to make them so sad.

She soon learned that what she thought was her baby doll in the fancy white box was her baby sister Pearl, whom they had all been eagerly waiting to come home from the hospital. Her dad had explained to her that baby Pearl had been sick, and even though she really wanted to stay with us, she could not, and she was going to be with the angels.

In her mind, she felt that because she opened the box when she was told not to, it was she who made everyone sad because baby Pearl was going to be with the angels. How could that be sad? When the Sunday School Lady told them about God and the angels, it sure sounded wonderful where they were. When she talked about going to our "Heavenly Home," it seemed like a beautiful place, and she wondered why it would be so sad if someone were going there.

She was standing outside the door peeking in, and she could see her dad sitting silently in the chair with his head cradled in his hands, allowing the tears to fall softly and silently. She had overheard the grownups talking earlier about a place called "the cemetery" where baby Pearl was going; she assumed that meant that she would sleep there until the angels came and got her. She had better make sure that Baby Pearl had a warm blanket. She would have to do what she could to fix things so no one would be sad. She had a plan forming already, but it was a secret. She sure wished she had a baby doll to tell the secret to.

That experience started my journey with grief, has undoubtedly shaped my life, and brought me to where I am today. We all have a story, and often, within that story, we find our true calling and purpose; I know this to be true in my case.

My story is a story of love, joy, loss, grief, and life after loss; it is a universal story. It is a story about finding your way, not about being a victim or a martyr; it is simply my story.

I was an inquisitive child; depending on who you ask, it might be annoying versus inquisitive. I did ask a lot of questions. Since Baby Pearl died, I have been looking at the world through old eyes; maybe I always did. I knew and felt things beyond my years; my grandma used to say I was an old soul but also a blessed one to have been gifted with a positive outlook and a great sense of humor, a family trait that has gotten me through some tough times.

After Baby Pearl, two other sisters died, and each time, I saw the face of grief and the toll it took on those left behind. I used to wonder how many times a heart can break; it is real, and if there is a point where it can no longer be patched.

When I was eight, my beautiful 49-year-old grandmother died unexpectedly, and again, I saw my dad being brought to his knees with grief. I saw the little boy inside, just needing his mom. But I also witnessed "one day, one moment, one breath" how the light gradually came back to his eyes, how he started to smile more, and the first time I heard him laugh was the most joyous sound I had ever heard. I came to understand that you can be sad, but within the sadness, there is hope, and the heart has an incredible capacity to heal. You can't heal what you can't feel.

My grandmother made me feel like the best little girl in the world, someone she was always overjoyed to see. She pretended not to notice when I used her lavender powder excessively; I always did, and she just said how lovely I smelled; to this day, I love lavender.

When I was ten, my maternal grandfather died, and I stood outside the bedroom door peeking in and saw my heartbroken mom; I saw a little girl crying for her dad, and I wondered again how many tears we are allotted and is there a point when we are all cried out. He used to let me fill his pipe, and it made me feel so important; the boys didn't even get to do that, and to this day, I love the smell of pipe tobacco.

What I have learned and know to be true is that death does not have the power to end our relationships, our love, or our hope. We do not simply close that chapter of our lives; instead, we integrate it into our future, and we take our loved ones with us. We find meaningful ways to commemorate them and keep the memories alive. Lilac bushes surround my house, and I feel her presence every time a gentle breeze brings her essence to me.

When I was 18, the rug was pulled out from under me when my vibrant, beautiful, funny mom, my best friend, was killed in a car accident. Now, I was the lost little girl who just needed her mom. My beautiful Aunt, who I adored, who was like a second mom, also died in the accident. Two amazing women in their 40s, ripped from their families.

I was lost in my own grief and deeply felt the devastation all around me, how my dad was brought to his knees yet again. I stood at the living room door for what felt like an eternity, just looking at him. He looked like he had looked all those years ago when I was little and saw him cry for the first time; he looked broken and lost.

For a moment, I wished I was that little five-year-old girl again. I needed her wisdom right now, and I so wished I had that same capacity to see it through those innocent eyes. I looked down at myself and realized for the first time that I was wearing red, the color my mom always loved on me, like the favorite red dress that I was wearing all those years ago when I formed my secret plan; maybe this was a sign from her that I could hang on to; "I'm here, you're not alone, I've got you."

I glanced to the right at the room where the Little White Box had been all those years ago; it seemed so much bigger then. Suddenly, I felt the feather-like brush of a small hand touch mine for a fleeting moment, and I knew that my guardian angel/baby doll was with me, and it gave me strength.

With silent tears running down his face, he said in the weakest voice I had ever heard the words that touched the deepest part of my soul, "She's gone." Two simple words forever etched in my memory.

I was awakened in the night by a sound that I knew only too well. I went to my little sister's room, stood at the door, and heard her crying softly. She was curled in a ball under the covers. I climbed into bed, got under the covers, held her so tight that she winched, and whispered, "It's okay, I'm here, I promise, I've got you."

She settled down and went to sleep. I lay awake for a long time holding her, whispering into the night, "Mom, if you can hear me, I'm going to need your help." As I drifted off to sleep, I heard a faint whisper that seemed to say, "It's okay. I'm here. I promise. I've got you."

I think there is a momentary stillness that accompanies devastating news. It is a stillness of the soul that seems to echo loss and grief across the ages. The stillness is an ethereal momentary reprieve from what's to come. Maybe it's God/the divine saying, "Take a moment, breathe; you will get through this; I've got you."

Many other losses followed over the years. The loss of my Nan was tough because she was my rock after my mom died and losing her felt like the last connection to my mom. When my incredible dad, my Rock, died suddenly a few years later, even after all the previous losses, I was blindsided. That little girl from all those years ago needed her dad.

My baby sister, who was eight when our mom died, lost her young husband to cancer. Late one night, I peeked in the door of his hospice room to see her curled up in the bed with him.

She looked like the little girl from all those years ago who had hidden under the covers to get away from her pain, and I felt helpless to comfort her this time.

I arrived at the hospital to see my best friend, my soul sister, and as I stood outside the door peeking in, with a knowing of what was to come, my first thought was, "I can't do this again," but that little voice said, "you can and will."

"Oh my heart, I knew you would come," and we held each other and cried for what felt like an eternity. We cried for those two idealistic 18-year-olds who had met so long ago at boot camp, ready to change the world and so naive about life. We cried for all the plans we had made over the years, for not honoring time like we had meant to. We cried because her favorite stuffed animal, we called him her "service stuffy," "Bartholomew," was caught up in the wires she was attached to, and then we burst out laughing at the absurdity of it all.

Oh, we had some crazy adventures over the years. Suddenly, we were in bouts of laughter, remembering crazy things like the cherry brandy incident and whose bad idea that had been!! We had proclaimed at 18, in our infinite wisdom, that we knew how we would die, but now we agreed that clearly God had other ideas.

As we sat there reminiscing between bouts of tears and laughter, we concluded that God had put us together all those years ago, from all the girls all over the country he put us two together, that we were meant to see each other through the good and the bad. At the end of the day, we would not have wanted it any other way.

I will always miss her, but as I left her hospital room that day, I did so with a heavy heart but also a sense of comfort. "I'll be seeing you down the road, my beautiful soul sister." She loved red roses; they were her favorite. The day she died, I had been looking out the window towards my garden and saw something red. When I went to investigate, I was not surprised to see on the leafless brown stick remnants of what used to be a rose bush, two perfect red roses; I smiled and laughed with joy; her message was received.

I believed for a long time that my family was cursed, that loss and pain were our destiny, was my destiny. We were clearly dealing with some crazy karma and waiting for the next shoe to fall. I no longer believe that and now understand the randomness of death. People die every day; loss is a part of life. Where there is life, there is loss, and where there is loss, there is grief; the two go hand in hand; one does not exist without the other.

Regardless of the circumstances, the amount of losses, age, relationship, and cause, the bottom line is "My loss is not worse than your loss, and yours is not worse than mine. The pain is no different to the griever." "At least" is a phrase that should never be used with grievers: "At least your grandfather was old, my sister was young," it doesn't matter to the person feeling the loss.

What I have learned through my own journey, through my work and conversations with other grievers, as well as through training as a Certified Grief Educator, is that there are several different lanes in life and our road would be much easier if we stayed in our own lane. We can only control how we react to what happens in our lane; we have no control over what happens in God's lane.

My "Nan" said to me after her only daughter, my mom, died, "We grieve our loss, and then we go on living because life is for the living, not for forgetting because we carry them with us, but we must keep living our life, our story is not over."

For something as universal as grief, it can be so lonely. As a licensed Edu-Therapy Practitioner, I can effectively show people how it is possible to eliminate any sense of isolation they may be feeling so that they can discover how to experience life again. A group member of mine, who lost her husband of 30 years, shared, "I feel like a weight has been lifted; I can be with others with shared experience and not feel guilty about not being "the grieving widow" every minute." Another shared, "I didn't think that I would ever be able to talk about my loss freely; you learn to keep it inside because very few want to hear about it." They experienced what grievers want: their grief to be witnessed. Grievers are not broken or need to be fixed.

Garth Brooks said it best "I could have missed the pain, but I would have had to miss the dance". I know what it feels like to have little bits of your heart, soul and hope chipped away. I have turned my pain into purpose, to help others see that there is life after loss, that after the sorrow, there will be sunshine, and life is worth the dance; I know mine has been worth the dance and I would not have wanted to have missed a single moment with my loved ones. "It's the heart afraid of breaking that never learns to dance, and the soul afraid of dying that never learns to live." Bette Midler.

Someone recently asked me how I knew when I was done grieving, and my answer was, "I'll let you know if that happens."

We will always grieve the loss of a loved one; I've heard it said many times that grief is the price we pay for love. Loss is part of life; death is random, and we are not being punished or cursed. Being able to remember our loved ones without the intense pain is when we know that we have started to heal.

Golden Nugget

"There is life after loss. I do not believe that death has the power to end our relationships, end our love or end our hope. We often think there is no way to heal from loss but we start to heal when we can remember our loved ones with more love than pain."

About Author:

Name – Marie Bailey

Contact – https://www.facebook.com/groups/1118934928772305/

I'm Marie, "I am a Heartfelt Grief Guide, committed to walking with you while you navigate the rocky waters of the Grieving Process, from Sorrow to Sunshine".

As a Certified Grief Educator and a Licensed Edu-Therapy Practioner, I help grievers see that there is life after loss. For something as universal as grief, it can be very lonely. I show clients how it is possible through a process called Edu-Therapy "Healing Your Heart" to effectively eliminate any sense of isolation they may be feeling, so that they can discover how to fully experience life again.

Chapter 20

Mary J Robinson
The Heart of a Woman

Some moments in our lives are so vivid that they stick with us for a lifetime. Moments such as these can invoke lingering sadness, spiraling excitement, or enlightening lessons. Regardless of the result, their messages are impossible to ignore. I've had more than a few defining moments in my life, and I've come to realize that every pivotal occurrence enhances my perspective. Here's my story:

When I was young, I always knew I wanted to help people. I remember pretending to be a teacher with my friends. We had an entire school set up in the basement: chalkboard, chalk, and small tables with chairs – it felt like a real classroom. The tiny seed I planted as a child stayed with me over the years. In 2001, I earned my bachelor's degree with a double major in elementary education and mild to moderate disabilities. In 2008, I attained my master's degree in special education, emphasizing visual impairments, and was hired as a teacher of the visually impaired. God had a plan for me, and through it all, He remained by my side. Little did I know exactly what He had in mind for my future until my BIG project... The Sensory Courtyard, where "Seeds Sown Today Bring Blossoms Tomorrow."

In the summer of 2011, a 'chance' encounter at a convention in Florida changed my life's direction. While there, I met a family with a three-year-old boy who was blind. His mother told me about his difficulties in developing skills and reaching important milestones. I discovered that her son was very tactile-defensive, meaning he did not want to touch anything, let alone play with toys. Often, the three-year-old sat in a corner crying when early interventionists came into their home to work on needed skills. His mother decided to plant a garden in her backyard with her son, even though he demonstrated no desire to be involved. Regardless of his attitude, she exposed him to the garden daily, introducing him to the assortment of plants. Over time, he began touching, picking, smelling, and tasting the vegetation. As the early interventionists continued to work with her son, he began to explore! He started reaching important milestones as these tactile defensive traits diminished, and the educational gap began shrinking to a realistic size.

After meeting that family in Florida, a spark grew inside me. I thought, "If that mother could do this for her son from a simple garden in their backyard, then why couldn't I do something in an educational setting with specialized interactive areas? Each space would spark the senses differently to help students of ALL abilities." This dream invigorated me. I wanted to give a voice to those who could not speak for themselves and those who require alternate avenues or paths to learn, grow, and achieve.

That short visit with the boy's mother was a significant turning point in my life. Was it *really* 'chance' that led to my passion project called the Sensory Courtyard? Looking back, I know this project was more significant than myself – the universe guided it. Everything lined up just as it was supposed to, and I could feel God smiling down on my plan. This doesn't mean everything was clear to me initially, though. It's easy to see these events and label them as fortunate when you look back through time, but at the moment, I needed to have all my senses on board.

When I first conceptualized the vision of the Sensory Courtyard, it felt unreal, as if it was just a fantasy. How could I bring something like this to fruition? Fantasies are not transformed into reality overnight. In my case, the Sensory Courtyard took three years. And, like many plans, it had some ups and downs. Despite challenges, the signs that God placed in my path assured me He was by my side.

As days turned into years, construction continued on the 3,000-square-foot project. I had also been working behind the scenes, using presentations and grant applications to raise funds. I put my heart and soul into this dream, and it showed. We planned to have an open house in August 2014. Completion of the Sensory Courtyard was near.

It was the end of the 2013-14 school year, and I was beyond ready for summer break. I was irritable and worn out after a hectic year managing student needs, overseeing the construction of the Sensory Courtyard, and fitting in quality time with family. Little did I know that my aspirations would take a dramatic detour if I wanted to be alive when they were finished. The sudden diagnosis of acute myeloid leukemia was utterly heartbreaking and unexpected. Thankfully, my school district was incredibly supportive, and they postponed the grand opening until I returned to work the following year.

As anyone could guess, this gave me much time to meditate and reflect on my life choices and inner strength. I prayed for peace, understanding, and wisdom. I also prayed for courage to have the ultimate trust in God to get me through this. I told myself I was not a victim of CANcer. After all, no matter what happens in the end, we are always victors because of the blood of Jesus. I knew Heaven would be waiting if my time was done on Earth.

My CANcer journey is one of the many life-altering events that invoked a shift in direction. In August 2014, I knew something was wrong with me, and I was scared. I had spent the past three years engrossed in my career and passion project, the

Sensory Courtyard, a magical enclosed space aiding in the progression of developmental milestones for those of all abilities. However, as I continued to work, I began to feel tired. On top of this fatigue, I also noticed changes in my body that didn't seem normal. I am the type of person who keeps commitments and pushes through difficult situations, so although I knew something wasn't right, I kept up with my work and home routines. Unfortunately, the lack of energy was only getting worse.

The whirlwind that took hold of me began when I visited my family doctor on August 4, 2014, and asked for bloodwork. I received the doctor's phone call the next day with the results. He said I had a condition known as pancytopenia. This is when white and red blood cells and platelets are low. He immediately scheduled an appointment with an oncologist. My new oncologist ordered additional blood work and scheduled a bone marrow biopsy on the following day.

On August 12, I was diagnosed with acute myeloid leukemia, an aggressive type of leukemia. Statistically, I had a fifty-percent chance of survival. As I sat with my husband, Tim, in the doctor's office, my emotions spiraled uncontrollably. My doctor compassionately told me he wished it was a less aggressive type of leukemia to tackle and overcome. He said I could do it, but the road ahead would be full of potholes and loose gravel. I turned to my husband and, with a mask of tear-filled confidence, told him I was in the fifty-percent bracket of survival.

The following words from my doctor's mouth hit me hard: without immediate chemotherapy treatments, I would have only a few months left to live. My whole life flashed before me, and I thought of my children. I wanted to raise and shape them into respectable, hardworking, honest adults. I longed to experience their high school graduations, weddings, and births of their children. I wanted it *all* – I wanted LIFE! Additionally, my three-year-long project, the Sensory Courtyard, was nearing completion.

When I managed to take control of the disarray around me, I looked straight up to heaven and pleadingly prayed for God to have mercy on me. The only thing I could do at that moment was grab onto faith, so that's what I did. I wiped my tears and decided right then to fight this disease with everything I had. At that moment, I realized just how strong I am.

I knew there would be good days and bad days, but my focus was on the future. In my mind, this diagnosis was just temporary, and it totally sucked, but I had God in the ring with me, ready to take swings anytime I didn't have the strength to do so on my own. I was ready and willing. I also knew I had my family, friends, and community to pray for my survival – this made all the difference.

On August 13, I admitted myself into the hospital to begin the scariest process in my entire life. I knew whatever was to come would be extremely hard and painful, but I chose to proceed so that I could live. I was thankful for this chance. People are killed in accidents in an instant on a daily basis. At least I had an option. I choose LIFE.

God doesn't wish for bad things to happen to people, but He does find extraordinary ways to help people get through tough times. I went through all the chemotherapy treatments necessary for remission and experienced many miracles in the process. My team of doctors did not think the cancer would come back. The battle was won through the Grace of God.

In August 2015, I returned to work full-time and slowly got back into a hectic, busy lifestyle. Leukemia had become a distant memory. We had a successful open house for the Sensory Courtyard, and it was a dream come true. I felt on top of my game and continued with 6-month routine checkups. Life was good.

Shortly after that, Tim and I became involved in a twelve-week program called *A Time to Heal*. This program is for cancer patients who have completed treatments and for their caregivers. It's designed to provide support while recovering from cancer and offers encouragement for the person caring for you. One presenter, in particular, came to the discussion group and talked about ways to calm yourself or others. She had extensive knowledge about healing your inner core and provided information about the healing modality of Reiki – a Japanese technique for stress reduction and relaxation that also promotes healing. This marked the beginning of my journey towards learning more about healing energy. I took many courses over the next few years, as well as participating in a two-year herbalist program.

In May 2017, the time arrived to draw blood for labs during a routine checkup. I noticed a pool of blood around the needle and said something to Tim, but he said not to worry. I tried to brush off my anxiousness as we waited to see my doctor for the lab results. The conclusions were very alarming. My blood counts were considerably lower than they had been in the past. This was not expected at all! My doctor gave the devastating news that the leukemia had returned. This time, unlike the last, I would need a stem cell transplant from a donor if I wanted long-term survival and a cure. This meant I had to leave my current oncologist and hospital family, whom I loved, and join a new one that had the facility fit for allogeneic stem cell transplants.

When bad things happen, we are given opportunities to reflect and learn from them. I learned techniques throughout my past CANcer journey. I committed myself to doing whatever it takes to get through this.

I spent several weeks in the hospital during chemotherapy treatments. Just like last time, there were signs I was going to make it through. I found out the intense chemo put me into remission after a bone marrow biopsy and aspiration. I started wondering if I'd ever find a suitable donor for a stem cell transplant that would cure me for good. *Be the Match* searched worldwide and found three 10 out of 10 matches. My doctor chose a male with blood type A Positive as my match. After the stem cell transplant, my blood type would gradually shift to the donor's type. I knew this final stage for long-term wellness would have a positive outcome. I just needed to let my heart lead the way and prevent fearful thoughts from taking over.

August 15 arrived, and I was admitted to the hospital. The transplant was a frightening roller coaster of a ride. I needed many blood and platelet transfusions throughout the treatments, just as before. Nausea and vomiting were a daily occurrence for months. My groin area, neck, armpits, hands, and feet turned dark purple, burned, itched, blistered, and peeled. All of my fingernails and a couple of toenails also felt the wrath of chemo. Each of them broke away from my cuticle and slowly fell off. I was told the rashes on my arms were due to graft-versus-host disease, and I was put on steroids and cream for a short time. No matter the struggles, I always had my eye on the prize: good health and a long life with my family.

The 100 days of isolation were critical for staying healthy. I had to be carefully monitored to ensure the best outcome. When I was released, I spent months on the couch, feeling extremely tired and unwell. This last stage of healing was the most difficult, reminding me of how precious life is and the pain one will endure to survive.

At the 100-day mark, a bone marrow biopsy confirmed that I accepted 100% of the donor cells and had male DNA. My blood type changed to A Positive, and there was no sign of leukemia. The stem cell transplant was a success! After getting out of the hospital, I went from going to the doctor twice a week to eventually going once a year.

In September 2019, my donor shared his contact information, and we connected through email. My ultimate closure of this journey opened doors I didn't even know were there, including those of universal energy through modalities of Reiki, the Herbalist Program, and Healing Touch.

After undergoing the stem cell transplant and surpassing two near-death experiences, I have become very in tune with my body. There was a time when I was unable to understand why anyone had to suffer through trials, but now I know the answer:

everything God creates has a purpose. This stretch of suffering led to my growth in faith. When asked about my other passion for helping others, the answer is simple: Universal energy. I love to help others by tapping into the light of the universe and offering support. And it's crazy to think I would never have discovered natural healing without the stepping stone of CANcer. I am so happy Reiki and Healing Touch led me to a newfound state of contentment.

I am CURED! What an extraordinary feeling it holds. And I'm going to bloom where I'm planted.

These moments have led me to discover my superpower: mental fortitude. I am a maven of mental strength, resilience, and perseverance, and it's captured in my book "Seed, Stem, Bloom: Lessons From My Faith-led Journey Through CANcer." My deep hope is that SEED, STEM, BLOOM, brings comfort and offers guidance to others going through similar life struggles. Perhaps the valuable lessons I learned along the way will spark life in another soul. May God bless you on your journey.

Golden Nugget

"A life with meaning is a life worth living."
~ Mary J Robinson

About Author:

Name – Mary J Robinson
Contact – https://www.kaleidoscopeenergy.com/

Mary J Robinson is a dedicated warrior against adversity and an expert in teaching students with visual impairments. She faced acute myeloid leukemia twice, deepening her commitment to life and inspiring others through her journey chronicled in "Seed, Stem, Bloom: Lessons From My Faith-led Journey Through CANcer." Her resilience, fueled by love, faith, and support, embodies the power of a positive mindset and determination.

About the Author

Sanet Van Breda from Johannesburg South Africa

President of Your Voice TV Network/Producer/ Publisher/ Author/Speaker/ Mentor.

The voice of millions, providing space and stages for extraordinary souls to illuminate our world with their brilliance, wisdom, and transformative stories across all my platforms, TV shows, Diamond Moments Magazine, Soul Diamond Publishers and MWAH Production. My mission is dedicated to empowering communities, particularly Diamond Beauties Forever and Tanzanite Heroes.

My Golden Nugget has not only saved my life but has also sent me in a direction to passionately follow my purpose for life. "If your WHY is big enough, you can do anything and everything!"

By connecting my heart to my voice, I have discovered great power. Living in the present moment daily, I am able to showcase my beautiful community, highlighting that they are truly amazing, beautiful, loved, and enough (ABLE). Your story matters, your voice lives because it has life, and your words will serve their purpose. Speak life with LOVE!

Thank you for being courageous every day—showing up for yourself and others, stepping up to take action in your personal life, your business, your family, and your community. When you are ready, soul up and live with intention and purpose. Take care of yourself, smile often, and keep on dancing. Mwah!

Diamond Beauties Forever(Women)
https://www.facebook.com/groups/diamondbeautiesforever
Tanzanite Hero (Men)
https://www.facebook.com/groups/965904067362902

Diamond Moments Magazine:
https://selflove4me.com/diamond-moments-issue-4/

Newsletter: https://selflove4me.com/
SLIM Page: https://www.facebook.com/selflove4me/
Facebook: https://www.facebook.com/sanet.vanbreda.3/
YouTube: https://www.youtube.com/channel/
    UC83ghcloVejxKJ8oAAZeEaA
Instagram: https://www.instagram.com/sanetvanbreda/
LinkedIn: https://www.linkedin.com/in/sanet-van-breda
TikTok: https://www.tiktok.com/@sanetvanbreda
Twitter: https://twitter.com/SanetVanBreda
Pinterest: https://za.pinterest.com/sanetvbreda20/

The Unbreakable Bond of the Diamond Beauties

Poem by Sanet van Breda

When women stand together,
A force is born, unlike any other.
With hands clasped and hearts united,
The world can be changed, we are reminded.
We lift each other up,
Supporting and cheering every step.
Our bond is unbreakable,
Our resilience unmistakable.
We shine brighter together,
Our light magnified forever.
Through trials and triumphs,
We hold each other up.
So let us stand tall,
In solidarity and with a call.
For Diamond Beauties standing together,
Can change the world forever.

www.selflove4me.com

Made in the USA
Middletown, DE
28 June 2024

56509557R00133